AMERICAN HERITAGE

August, 1972 · Volume XXIII, Number 5

LETTER FROM THE EDITOR

The life of a radical in the old days was hard and dangerous. He was rarely successful and tended more often to wind up badly—he was jailed, run out of town, laughed at, or, worst of all, ignored. But in modern times we have changed all that. We listen, which may be the root of the problem, and we adopt the scheme in question at once, however harebrained. The theme is "instant acceptance." It happens steadily. Just the other day it was pants for women, and then long hair for men. One minute little Willie had a shaggy head and a wisp of a new beard, and within six months even old men were hiding their ears behind large, fluffy sideburns and their collars under gray pageboys. Somebody suggested that Ms. would be a fine form of address for the liberated woman who does not want to reveal what used to be called her "condition" as either spinster or married woman. Now mail floods into this office addressing as Ms. a great many women who previously saw no objection to being either Miss or Mrs. The surrender outruns the attack.

Much the same thing can be found daily in anyone's morning paper. Homosexuals demonstrate, just as though they were Teamsters, or Italian-Americans, or welfare recipients, and the Establishment falls on its knees. And so Yale gets an officially recognized Gay Alliance, probably next door to Skull and Bones, and no skeletons are hidden. A similar corporal's guard of liberated women, or militant blacks, or rioting students can produce the same effect. Businessmen crumble, city councillors tremble, faculties cave in. Those who resist are denounced; the *New York Times* recently called one group of holdouts "self-appointed upholders of 'the old virtues'" (which leads one to wonder, disloyally, who appointed the *New York Times*, and to what).

It is a great time, one has to admit, to be on the bandwagon of radical change, and it is obvious that nothing—old virtue, old idea, even old landmark—is going to escape. With thoughts like these in mind, we picked up a recent issue of *Preservation News*, the esteemed publication of The National Trust for Historic Preservation, which devotes itself to fighting the battle against the bulldozer and the builder. The Trust, which is one of the few remaining American organizations with a bit of backbone left, reproduces the little picture shown here, depicting Faneuil Hall, one of the birthplaces of our liberty, as it will look when an enormous forty-four-story office building is completed beside it. There's radical change for you. Since one other big building has already been erected behind it, and Boston's hideous new City Hall has gone up across the square (far right), the old hall will be effectively hemmed in. Boston has asked the U.S. Department of Housing and Urban Development (HUD) to approve the new structure, and we are sorry to say that despite some opposition, it obtained the approval of, of all things, the Massachusetts Historical Commission. As one local official, the Honorable John F. X. Davoren, commented, the historic structures would be no less historic "in shadow than in light." Here is a project, certainly, to match the proposed 307-foot observation tower overlooking the battlefield of Gettysburg, both in taste and monumentality.

It is easy enough to tear down what the pitiful handful of reactionaries like us regards as beautiful old buildings, as any official of HUD can tell you. The scars of HUD's achievements pockmark the country. But if it is merely expensive to engineer simple destruction, it takes skill and imagination to erect true enormities. To help out in any shortage of ideas, we have a store of ready-made enormities to suggest for any locality in need of one. Here are a few samples:

1. *The Top-out Cop-out:* In this beautifully designed plan, the amenity to be preserved—say, Independence Hall, Philadelphia—is lifted up and dropped on the top of an eighty-story building, thus enshrining it in a position where it can overawe lovers of liberty within a radius of several hundred miles, in smog-free periods.

2. *Forever Amber:* This scheme involves embedding an entire district—say, Beacon Hill, Boston, or the Battery in Charleston—in clear or tinted fireproof plastic, thus preserving it like baby's bronzed booties and at the same time keeping out undesirable elements. Aluminum walkways entirely encircle the preserved area and are washed down nightly by electronic means with a substance that removes all traces of graffiti.

3. *The Disney:* In this method, the landmark in question—say, Bunker Hill—is surrounded with an amusement park on the order of Disneyland. Cunningly devised monorails carry the visitor back and forth between the lines of simulated redcoats and patriots, clever mechanized figures that re-enact the battle every two hours so realistically that many of the patrons must be taken away fainting to local first-aid stations, although medical attention would be included in the admission charge.

4. *The Cloverleaf:* Since the modern American spends hours of his time on superhighways, and most of that circling on and off cloverleafs, it is clear that maximum attendance can be expected if these are situated at historic points like Plymouth Rock or the Alamo. Let us not forget what Dr. Johnson said in his *Journey to the Western Isles of Scotland:* "That man is little to be envied, whose patriotism would not gain force upon the plain of Marathon, or whose piety would not grow warmer among the ruins of Iona." Imagine one cloverleaf twisting around the White House, so that tourists can be inspired with intimate views of the Executive Mansion while they circle it again and again, hunting for exits. In order not to disturb the privacy of the Presidential family, no exit would actually lead anywhere except back onto the throughway.

We have a great many more schemes like these available, of course, for in revolutionary times one should always be a few surrenders ahead of the attackers.
—*Oliver Jensen*

AMERICAN HERITAGE

The Magazine of History

SENIOR EDITOR
Bruce Catton

EDITOR
Oliver Jensen

ARTICLES EDITOR
E. M. Halliday

EXECUTIVE EDITOR
Nat Brandt

ASSOCIATE EDITORS
Barbara Klaw Bernard A. Weisberger

ART DIRECTOR
Emma Landau

PICTURE EDITORS
Carla Davidson Mary Dawn Earley
ASSISTANT: Devorah Kanter

COPY EDITOR
Joyce O'Connor
ASSISTANT: Anne D. Steinhardt

CONSULTING EDITOR: Joan Paterson Kerr

CONTRIBUTING EDITOR: Robert C. Alberts

ADVISORY BOARD
Carl Carmer   Eric F. Goldman
Gerald Carson   Louis C. Jones
Henry Steele Commager   Alvin M. Josephy, Jr.
Marshall B. Davidson   Howard H. Peckham
John A. Garraty   Francis S. Ronalds
S. K. Stevens

AMERICAN HERITAGE PUBLISHING CO., INC.

PRESIDENT AND PUBLISHER
Paul Gottlieb
EDITOR IN CHIEF
Joseph J. Thorndike
SENIOR EDITOR
Richard M. Ketchum
EDITORIAL ART DIRECTOR
Murray Belsky

AMERICAN HERITAGE is published every two months by American Heritage Publishing Co., Inc.; editorial and executive offices, 1221 Avenue of the Americas, New York, N.Y. 10020. Treasurer, Marjorie C. Dyer; Secretary, John C. Taylor III. Correspondence about subscriptions should be sent to American Heritage Subscription Office, 383 West Center Street, Marion, Ohio 43302. Single copies: $5.00. Annual subscriptions: $20.00 in U.S. and Canada; $21.00 elsewhere.

A ten-year Index covering Volumes VI–XV is available at $5.00, and a five-year Index of Volumes XVI–XX at $3.50.

AMERICAN HERITAGE will consider but assumes no responsibility for unsolicited materials. Title registered U.S. Patent Office. Second-class postage paid at New York, N.Y., and at additional mailing offices.

Sponsored by
American Association for State & Local History · Society of American Historians

CONTENTS *August, 1972 · Volume XXIII, Number 5*

COVER: "Americans have tried, variously, to trade with China, to 'open' China, to convert China, to exploit China, to punish China, to assist China, to modernize China, to defend China, and most recently to 'contain' and isolate China." So says the author of our survey of Chinese-American relations that starts on the following page; and our cover picture is a detail from a painting, reproduced in its entirety on pages 24–25, suggesting the first and perhaps the happiest of these many efforts. The painting depicts the whole process of tea production from bush to packing case; it was done by an unknown British artist and now belongs to the Huntington Hartford Collection. *Back cover:* Paul Morphy, possibly the greatest American chess champion of all time, whose story is told on pages 48–49, was twenty-two when he received this admiring dedication in the book *The First American Chess Congress*, published in New York in 1859.

A CYCLE OF CATHAY

President Nixon's visit to Peking starts one more surprising turn in an American=Chinese "affair" nearly two centuries old

Richard Nixon's twenty-thousand-mile pilgrimage to the center of Chinese civilization—"the week that changed the world," as he put it—may not actually have changed the world, though it quite probably did turn a new page in world history by making it unlikely that the international politics of East Asia, at least, will ever be the same again.

But whatever their global effect, one thing the Kissinger-Nixon bold strokes of 1971-72 most strikingly *did* do was to open a new chapter in that small but curious subdivision of world history, the 188-year-old tale of Chinese-American relations.

To put the matter simply, America's existence is relatively short and special, China's existence extremely long but also special; and these two very different peoples—Americans and Chinese—have had an increasingly intense and complex relationship with each other over much of the past two centuries.

Americans have tried, variously, to trade with China, to "open" China, to convert China, to exploit China, to punish China, to assist China, to modernize China, to defend China, and most recently to "contain" and iso-late China. The reverse of the relationship—Chinese feelings, at various times, about America the intruder, the exploiter, the imperialist, the friend, the hope, the disappointment, and the archenemy—has been less intense, since Americans were only one foreign element among many in China, though nonetheless significant.

Historians have found it especially hard to explain the persistence of a virtual China obsession among influential groups of Americans from our earliest days right up through the week of the Nixon trip. They have found it even harder to explain the notable swings, the violent ups and downs, in American attitudes toward China.

One shrewd observer of both China and America, the M.I.T. political scientist Harold R. Isaacs, has identified at least six separate phases of U.S. response to China. The eighteenth century and the first years of the nineteenth, he concludes, were an "Age of Respect"—when Americans were in awe of the Confucian empire's splendor, its exports, and even its elaborate system of governance. This was followed, between the Opium War and the turn of this century, by an "Age of Contempt"—when Americans were generally more struck by the backwardness,

By JAMES C. THOMSON, JR.

4

weakness, and conservatism of the decaying empire. Then came an "Age of Benevolence," roughly between 1905 and 1937, as the empire tried to reform, collapsed, and gave way to a republic under such Western-oriented leaders as Sun Yat-sen and Chiang Kai-shek. In this period Americans sensed a great opportunity to serve as guides for the emerging new China.

With the coming of the Sino-Japanese War, Isaacs continues, a new "Age of Admiration" took hold—a period in which China's struggle against the Japanese invaders fired American imaginations; Madame Chiang Kai-shek's triumphal visit to the United States in 1943 was the high-water mark of that phase. It was quickly followed, however, by an "Age of Disenchantment," from 1944 to 1949, when the glaring deficiencies of the war-weary Nationalist government were revealed in its abortive effort to turn back the Communist revolution. Finally, after 1949, an "Age of Hostility" toward China's new Communist rulers set in, intensified by both a sense of betrayal and the passions of the Korean War.

Reflections on the Sino-American relationship bring one back, inevitably, to the context of the Nixon trip: not just China's experience of Americans (and vice versa) but China's experience of foreigners in general, foreigners' experience of China, and, specifically, the traditions of executive tourism on Chinese soil.

To begin with the last point, the President's journey was only the latest in a very long record of visitations by foreign rulers and their emissaries to the Middle Kingdom and sometimes, if they were lucky, to the Forbidden City itself. Despite Mr. Nixon's good fortune, it has not been an entirely happy chronicle.

Take the case of one Thomas Pires, an early Portuguese ambassador who sought in 1517 to pry open the Chinese door. Pires got off on the wrong foot initially by firing a courtesy salute with cannon in Canton harbor, for which the unflattered Chinese officials promptly demanded an apology. He then came ashore accompanied by a blast of trumpets, for which another apology was immediately demanded. And he politely offered gifts to the authorities—which were duly noted as "tribute" from Portugal, a place listed as somewhere "south of Java."

Thomas Pires eventually got to his goal, the imperial throne in Peking (though as Sino-Portuguese relations turned sour, he had the later misfortune to die in a Canton prison). Pires thereby became the first Westerner of the modern era to undergo a ritual that required, it seems, considerable athletic prowess: the performance of the kowtow (or *k'o t'ou*), a ceremonial approach to the emperor that involved three kneelings interspersed with a total of nine full prostrations ("head-bangings"). It was a performance that undoubtedly left its performers both breathless and humbled.

All this was basically ceremonial recognition of what was, to the Chinese, obvious: that China *was* the center of the known earth, an advanced and ancient civilization adjacent to the much more backward peoples of north, central, and southeast Asia, and that access to China's benevolence and material goods required submissiveness and good manners in the Chinese style.

Of course, the proud and sturdy Englishmen of the eighteenth and early nineteenth centuries who sought to open China to trade and diplomacy regarded such ceremonies as distinctly un-English. But even when they refused to undergo them, lesser pitfalls still lurked on the road to Peking. There is no evidence, for instance, that Lord Macartney, the Briton who tried to force diplomatic relations on the Chinese empire in 1793, could read the inscriptions on the stately pennants that the Chinese placed on his vehicles as he journeyed to the capital: "Ambassador bearing tribute from the country of England." Macartney's visit was thereby recorded as a mission of homage from a vassal state; the Ch'ien-lung emperor commended George III for his "respectful spirit of submission" but pointed out that "our celestial empire possesses all things in prolific abundance" and therefore needed no foreign contacts. Years of increasingly violent misunderstanding ensued, until the Opium War clarified the issue. In it, British naval firepower as of 1842 forced the Chinese to open several new ports besides Canton to "barbarian" traders.

As for official Americans, very late arrivals on the scene, their habit was generally to let Europeans run interference for them. An American executive who finally made it to Peking was former Massachusetts congressman Anson Burlingame, who became Washington's first full-fledged minister to China in 1861. Burlingame's virtue was good will, his failing a silver tongue. He was so genial and persuasive that he was appointed, on his retirement in 1868, China's first official envoy to the Western world and embarked, with two Chinese colleagues, on an extended mission to America, Britain, France, Germany, and Russia (where he suddenly expired in 1870). In this curious role Burlingame established (and indeed pre-empted) the euphoric tradition of Sino-American relations. "China," he declaimed to a rapt New York audience in 1867, "is willing to trade with you, to buy of you, to sell to you. . . . She invites your merchants, she invites your missionaries. She tells the latter to plant the shining cross on every hill and in every valley. The imagination kindles at the future which may be, and which will be, if you will be fair and just to China." Hard on the heels of Burlingame's words came the Tientsin massacre of foreign missionaries and thirty years of Chinese antiforeign agitation that culmi-

Dreams of wealth in the China trade sometimes ended disastrously, as the crew of the American trader President Adams *is discovering in this dramatic painting by an unknown Chinese artist about 1812.*

nated in the Boxer Rebellion. But the Burlingame syndrome of great expectations survives to this day.

By 1879, when ex-President Grant, travelling around the world one month out of office, became the first American Chief Executive (present or former) to visit China, things in Peking had loosened up a good deal. Gone, for Western visitors at least, were the kowtow and the concept of tribute, for the Chinese empire was now effectively shackled by the unequal treaties imposed by the West in the aftermath of their repeated use of superior military force. General Grant seems to have come and gone without incident.

Misunderstandings did persist, however, in the later record of Sino-American visitations. There is, for instance, the case of General Patrick J. Hurley, Franklin D. Roosevelt's personal representative to China, who arrived at the Yenan airstrip to confer with Mao Tse-tung in 1944 and, on emerging from his plane, delivered himself—in Oklahoma fashion—of a Choctaw war whoop. At which the party of welcoming officials is said to have dispersed temporarily in alarm. General Hurley's idiosyncrasies had a more lasting effect on history: he careened onward to bungle and destroy a promising American relationship with the Chinese Communists and then, through reckless charges as he resigned in 1945, sowed the first seeds of the poisonous "Who Lost China" debate back home.

So the tradition of high-level visitation to China is an uneven one, and Mr. Nixon—who graciously ended what Hurley had begun—can be grateful to have come and gone without giving or receiving major insult or injury.

But there is, of course, a far more important context to America's recent rediscovery of China than the fate of high-ranking official visitors, and that is the complex matter of what is called, in the new idiom, people-to-people relations.

From its earliest phases and throughout, the American–East Asian relationship was primarily the product of Americans who travelled to Asia in nongovernmental roles. To be sure, Asians came to America, too—as laborers in fairly large numbers, until they were eventually excluded, and also as students, diplomats, and immigrants—and their presence helped shape events on both sides of the ocean. But the dominant fact was the American thrust toward Asia, a thrust impelled by what some have termed the "acquisitive spirit."

What was to be acquired? Initially, from the 1780's, and to some extent throughout, Asian goods—wealth from the China trade. Early, too, from the second decade of the nineteenth century, Asian converts for Christianity. Toward the end of the century two additional objectives joined the acquisition list: Asian customers for the products of American industry as well as Asian conces-

Americans were active in the illicit opium trade. A key spot was this harbor off the island of Lin Tin, near Canton, where the drug was stored in hulks and then smuggled ashore with Chinese connivance.

sions for investors, and—for some dreamers of American empire—Asian bases to sustain American trading vessels and an expanded navy.

Traders, missionaries, industrialists, investors, entrepreneurs, navalists—these were the people who went west to Asia. And with them, very soon, came their protectors, the agents of the state: consuls, diplomats, and service attachés. With commerce and evangelism came the flag, and with the flag came the state.

It is hardly surprising that from earliest times the focal point was China. India belonged to Britain, and much of Southeast Asia fell within European colonial spheres. Japan, until midcentury, was tightly closed to intruders. Furthermore, Southeast Asia and Japan were fringes on the larger fabric of Chinese civilization. China was the heartland, very old, often powerful, fabled from time to time in the West. For readers in early America the most recent works on China were those of the eighteenth-century French philosophes. China was the center of Asia's population, culture, and trade in exotic goods.

People-to-people relations with China seem to have begun in 1784, just after the end of our war for independence, when the *Empress of China*, six months out of New York, arrived off the Portuguese colony of Macao, near Canton, on August 23 to become the first ship of American registry to participate in the China trade. Upon her return to New York in May, 1785, she had

netted a profit of 25 per cent on an investment of $120,000 —not enormous, but a clear promise of things to come.

What that vessel and its successors joined was a system of tightly controlled access to China that had evolved since the early eighteenth century. Contemptuous of merchants and suspicious of "barbarians" (i.e., foreigners), China's Confucian rulers had sought to restrict the sea barbarians to Canton as they did their overland counterparts, coming across Central Asia in the Marco Polo tradition, to designated market points in the north and northwest. At Canton, American traders from New York and New England—especially from Salem and Boston—joined trading representatives, or factors, from a half dozen or more European nations in inhabiting a series of "factories," or combined bachelor quarters and warehouses. These were in a riverfront section to which foreigners were confined outside the walled Chinese city. (Foreign wives were confined considerably farther away, in Macao; incentives to linger in Canton, once the trading season was over, were thus minimal—unless, of course, one wanted to escape one's wife.)

This Canton system of trade provided adventure for the young, the restless, and the brave, profits for merchant investors, and delights for those back home who had a taste for Chinese silks, porcelain, and teas. Much of the happy lore of the old China trade dates from this era. Not only did the foreigners have much to win—and sometimes lose. Chinese middlemen—the famous Hong (or business-firm) merchants, who "secured," or acted as guarantors for, each arriving foreign ship; the Co-Hong (or officially licensed merchant monopoly); and a wide assortment of compradors (accountants and foremen), "linguists" (interpreters), and supervisory officials—also developed deep and complex stakes in this regulated trade as well as in its darker side, smuggling, and also had much to win and lose.

These were the days when—as Samuel Eliot Morison has written—"Boston was the Spain, Salem the Portugal, in the race for Oriental opulence." Every Salem housewife had ambitions for a chest of hyson tea, a China silk gown, and a set of Canton chinaware. These were also the days of sudden and great prosperity for individuals and firms alike. By 1803 the Boston house of Perkins and Company had a representative in Canton and became, for a while, the oldest surviving American firm. In the next three decades the consolidation of various houses, including that of Perkins, led to the establishment of the leading American business in nineteenth-century China, Russell and Company, of Canton, originally founded by Samuel Russell of Middletown, Connecticut, in 1818— a firm that finally went under in 1891. Individuals as well as companies prospered. Between 1807 and 1827 the Canton agent of the Perkins-Sturgis-Forbes group, one John P. Cushing, with only two clerks to his establishment, did a business of millions of dollars a year—and returned a very wealthy man in 1830 to his Summer Street, Boston, mansion and his Belmont estate, attended by a retinue of Chinese servants. To cite one other individual of many: Warren Delano, one-time agent for Russell and Company, made not merely one but two major killings in the China trade in separate decades— and thereby gave his grandson, Franklin Delano Roosevelt, both a solid inheritance and a special sense of kinship with China.

A recurrent question, however, for the early American traders was how to pay for the much-desired tea, silks, and chinaware—and what to sell to the Chinese in exchange. For a while the answer was furs—especially from the North Pacific sea otter, whose skin was much prized by the Chinese upper class. For a time, sandalwood from Hawaii also found a market. By 1792 the trade route from New England to the Pacific Northwest coast to Canton and back to New England was fairly well established. But after 1815 a great change took place in such trade: a shift from silks and china to rapidly increasing quantities of teas transported to America and Europe.

At the root of the shift was the fact that tea, first known to Europe in the seventeenth century, had become in the course of the eighteenth century *the* British national beverage—an antidote, perhaps, to the clammy English climate. For a while heavily taxed (the cause, it will be recalled, of American boycotts, the Boston Tea Party, and thereby America's early turning toward coffee), it was nonetheless plainly a very great comfort that came to border upon addiction. After 1815, with the Napoleonic wars over, demand and supply could soar, with much to be carried, both to the United States and Europe, in American bottoms.

With that shift to tea in both cargo and volume, however, the need for something to provide in exchange became more acute. For a while Spanish silver dollars displaced sea-otter skins and sandalwood, declining in both supply and demand. But from 1827 onward, opium —long smuggled in, though not in large quantities—began to replace the Spanish dollars. Opium was compact, easy to conceal, didn't spoil—and the Chinese demand for it was sharply on the rise. Americans joined with their British cousins in importing the drug into China from India and the Near East. And the Chinese, both merchants and officials, connived with the foreigners to make the trade possible. (One must note, in passing, that history is at least symmetrical and retributive, now that the West, in the 1970's, finds itself assailed by massive illicit drug shipments from the Near East and Southeast Asia.)

The drug trade did create friction with the Chinese government, however, and, aside from the opium problem, deep tensions of various sorts were developing within the Canton system by the 1830's—tensions deriving mainly from an inherent clash between the free-trading ethic of an expansionist Great Britain, the leader of the Western thrust, and the self-isolating ethic of a proud and complacent government in Peking. One or the other eventually had to give, and in an unevenly matched combat over the proximate issue of opium import into China, it was the Chinese who gave way before the superior firepower of the foreigners.

America was not, at this juncture, a combatant. But when the first of the unequal treaties was imposed by Britain in 1842, United States commissioners moved in to demand their nation's share of the spoils on a "most-favored-nation" basis—meaning that they demanded henceforth any and all rights achieved by other powers, regardless of how they had been obtained. (The last vestige of these treaties was not finally given up by Washington until a century later, in 1943.)

Out of the unequal treaties there evolved, by 1860, an entirely new system of Sino-Western relations. Not only were foreigners given access to a large number of Chinese treaty ports on the coast and inland up the Yangtze River; they were also granted territorial concessions. In such ports, where foreign laws now prevailed, the outsiders were given immunity from Chinese

TEXT CONTINUES ON PAGE 89

WHEN WEST MET EAST

A Picture Portfolio

The first American ship to visit China was the *Empress of China*, which landed there in 1785; the *Empress*, anchored at Whampoa Reach, is one of the ships shown above on a fan brought back by her captain, John Green. From this date to the end of the nineteenth century, every American ship that returned from China was laden with cargoes of exotic Oriental commodities, especially teas and silks, the staples of the trade. Among the items most prized by the men who had lived and traded in the Orient were pictures and drawings of China and the Chinese. The alien and seemingly curious culture intrigued the Westerner, and hundreds of thousands of paintings and water colors of every phase of Chinese life, executed by Chinese artists who had learned to paint in the Western style, were brought to America. Views of Chinese figures and landscapes were painted on everything from fans to porcelains to meet the tremendous demand. The port views were the picture post cards of the day and accurately showed the families at home where their trader relatives had travelled and lived. Although many of the pictures reveal a distant and long-faded culture, some of the same street trades and occupations that were painted for the Americans in the nineteenth century can still be seen in Hong Kong and Macao. Today we look to our renewed contact with China with much the same fascination our ancestors felt almost two hundred years ago.

Our portfolio was assembled by Joan Paterson Kerr, with the cooperation of Carl L. Crossman of the Childs Gallery in Boston; he also supplied caption information. Mr. Crossman has a major book, *The China Trade*, based on long experience as a collector of China material, scheduled for publication in October by the Pyne Press.

Foreign vessels crowd Whampoa Reach around 1850 in a panoramic rendering by Youqua, finest among Chinese artists of the busy trading ports.

A tranquil Chinese garden shows two non-Oriental features: the lady with her baby and the Western lighting fixtures in the house at right.

The adventurous Miss Harriet Low, of Salem

A SHORT TETHER
FOR FOREIGNERS

Profiting from the needs of other American merchants, Thomas Hunt ran a floating chandlery at Whampoa Reach.

For foreign vessels the long trip to Canton ended when they dropped anchor at Whampoa, ten miles below the city. Supercargoes and captains then took small boats up to the Hongs, or trade warehouses. On the way they saw evidence of the enterprise of Salem, Massachusetts, in the schooners and storage hulks of Thomas Hunt's chandlery. Salem also provided a lively challenger of Chinese custom in the person of Harriet Low. Western women were banned from Canton, but Miss Low was unusually curious and resourceful. In 1832 she disguised herself as a boy and went up to the Hongs—a breach that, when discovered, temporarily set back Western trade. Harriet's portrait (above) was painted by the English artist George Chinnery, who had come to Macao in 1825 in flight from an inconvenient wife and creditors. He found the "no women in Canton" rule a blessing and hastily moved there when the wife followed him to China. (One of Chinnery's pupils, Lam Qua, became proficient enough in Western-style painting to exhibit at London's Royal Academy.) But Canton's days as a place where foreign men were exiled or protected from their women were numbered in 1832. By the 1850's Occidental ladies were freely visiting the once-banned area, seeing the sights, and, like the young mother opposite, enjoying the luxurious residences owned by the thriving Hong merchants.

11

Hong and residence of Augustine Heard and Company of Ipswich, Mass., in Shanghai in 1849

LURES OF A TRADER'S LIFE

Until the opening of the treaty ports in 1842, Westerners were required to live and trade in a small area outside the city of Canton, a location they found highly frustrating with its severe restrictions. At the end, of the business season they returned to Portuguese-owned Macao. The houses built later by the Americans in Hong Kong and Shanghai, however, were lavish and comfortable and possessed all the advantages of Western and Oriental culture combined. Although ordinary Chinese architecture was not highly picturesque, construction was sound.

Canton's waterfront in 1844 was lively. The boats in this painting seem to be Chinese, but there are signs of Western presence: the round

In 1807 Canton's Hongs faced a square that was one of the few places where the Chinese permitted men of all nations to meet. Against the backdrop of these sober façades, Chinese and foreign tradesmen strolled, argued, gossiped, bargained, and took one another's measure.

structures above and far right are Dutch and French forts, the white buildings far left are the Hongs. The sky area has been cropped.

About 1850 the Chinese painter Tingqua made this water color showing his shop-studio with its wares for sale to "barbarian" visitors.

A maker of firecrackers with his wares   *A street vendor of cakes and fruits*   *A decorator of lacquerware at work*

THE BUSY STREETS OF CANTON

American traders in Canton haunted the streets and alleys where the shops were located, in search of curiosities to bring home or send to relatives, friends, and clients in the United States. To these Yankees, such thoroughfares as Old and New China streets were full of vitality and of astonishing sights. Craftsmen and vendors hawked their goods in the open; entertainers performed acrobatic feats and sang, played, danced, or mimed for whatever they could pick up. More fascinating still was the practice in the Chinese judicial system of torturing and executing malefactors in public. Lacking the power of the modern tourist to record such scenes with the camera, the traders flocked to artists to purchase or commission water colors of the local sights or of the Hongs, or even portraits of themselves as seen by Chinese painters.

A tightrope dancer bouncing to a drumbeat

Ultimate warning: criminals' heads on display

CHILDS GALLERY, INC.

Entertainment: a sword-swallower in the act

Public torture was a cautionary spectacle.

CHILDS GALLERY, INC.

Pig-roasting in an outdoor oven

An exterminator with his poison pouch

Fanciful fans in the manufacturing stage

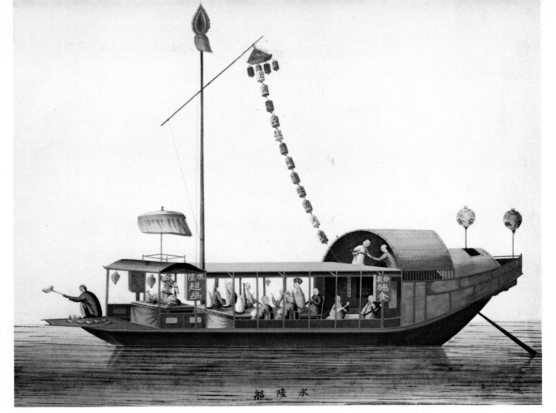

水陸船

In the waterborne ceremony above, chanting monks beseech gifts for the spirits of the dead. Below is probably a florist's yard, its rows of potted bonsai and flowering trees ready for some wealthy man's garden.

A mandarin and wife, painted on glass around 1856

CEREMONY, STYLE, AND ORNAMENT

The ceremonial richness of Chinese domestic, social, and business life was well represented in series of water colors depicting entertainment, household interiors, manufacturing, boating, parades, presentations, and music making. These, painted on English paper or on Chinese pith paper, were usually bound in sets and avidly purchased by Americans; occasionally other materials would be used for special subjects like the mandarin portraits above, painted on glass. One Chinese decorative art that became familiar to Americans was formal gardening. Rich Hong merchants like Houqua were proud to invite the Yankees to see their horticultural splendors in parks and terraces on the island of Honam, across the river from Canton, where acres of carefully attended gardens were embellished with pavilions, ponds, bridges, and gazebos. Typically, everything was hidden behind walls, a treatment that extended also to most private homes, whose grounds, however beautiful, were not open to the public gaze. The love of formal gardens made horticulture one of the better-paid occupations.

17

FORTUNES FROM
WORMS AND MUD

The sets of water colors most desired by Americans were those depicting the production and sale of the great staples of the trade with China—tea, porcelain, and silk. Each set had one or two dozen paintings, and sometimes two or more sets were bound together to furnish a record of economic history unique in attractiveness. Silk culture in China was possibly four thousand years old in the 1800's. It began with the nurture of silkworms on mulberry trees, like those in the middle picture, opposite page. After the worms had spun their cocoons, the delicate fibers were extracted, twisted together, dyed, and hung out to dry (bottom). Later they were woven into fabrics whose glossy beauty was so valued that numerous European countries tried hard to encourage local silk industries. But Chinese silk remained highly prized, and although China kept much of its raw silk for the home market, certain silk merchants, like Eshing (top), became rich in the trade—and so did some Americans.

Rice, though a humbler crop and hardly important to American traders, was far more vital in the entire Asian economy. Probably domesticated in India long before Buddha, it is still the staple food of half the world's population. Most rice in China was of the kind grown in marshy, flooded lands. (Northern Chinese, however, use wheat as their basic grain.) On trips around Canton, traders saw rice fields like those above and at right, tended by patient coolies and muddy water buffaloes.

Americans in the China trade were well aware of the fact that Chinese porcelain was considered the world's finest—and not surprisingly, for the art of its manufacture had flourished for hundreds of years. Early in the nineteenth century shipments of dishes, bowls, jars, vases, tiles, and figurines began to make up a substantial part of the trade, and American housewives grew used to referring to their dinnerware as "china." Porcelain shops near the Hongs, like the one above—whose sign promises the best porcelains from Kiangsi province—were full of bargain-hunting foreigners, just as similar shops in Hong Kong are today. Customers could have decorations made to order by Chinese artists who sometimes showed a charming lack of realism. On the vase opposite, custom-finished for a patriotic Yankee buyer with a scene of the signing of the Declaration of Independence, the members of the Continental Congress have a remarkably Oriental appearance.

ON MANY A VASE AND JAR

THE REWARDING CUP OF TEA

The commodity most eagerly sought by the Western merchant was tea, and it was for this Oriental luxury that traders risked lives, money, and vessels in the hope of amassing large fortunes. Chinese merchants grew wealthy in the same business: one of the best known, best liked, and richest was Houqua, whose portrait (opposite) was painted by the celebrated Chinese artist Lam Qua. His trademark, or chop, which appeared on the tea he sold, is shown above. The tea label to the right is from one of the large tea companies toward the end of the nineteenth century. The Hong area of Canton as it looked in 1855 is seen in the water color below, executed by Lam Qua's younger brother Tingqua; the key in the right margin identifies the companies in each of the buildings, including such American firms as Lindsay and Company, Heard and Company, Wetmore and Company, and the best known, Russell and Company. The writing is probably that of John Forbes, member of a distinguished American family of China traders.

OVERLEAF: *This comprehensive painting is a handsome and informative montage showing the raising, processing, and selling of tea from first step to last. The plant grows in the surrounding hills. In the various buildings workmen sort and sift the leaves and fire them (that is, dry them by heat). At left foreground, a supercargo bargains with a Chinese merchant to get a good price on the tea being packed and weighed behind them. A Chinese sign over the door declares that this is the righteousness-harmony shop. In the distance, ships wait to carry the tea westward.*

Decorative images

Iron spearhead

In 1965 widespread interest was excited by the first publication of a fifteenth-century map showing "Vinland" and purporting to be the earliest cartographic representation of any part of the North American continent. [See "Vinland the Good Emerges from the Mists," AMERICAN HERITAGE, October, 1965.] The Vinland Map tended to reinforce the conclusion long held by many historians that Leif Eiriksson (or Ericson) and other Vikings landed on the northeast coast of the continent around A.D. 1000. It did little if anything, however, to encourage the

The bleak vista above is believed to show Eric the Red's farm, near the southern tip of Greenland, from which Leif Eiriksson voyaged to Vinland around the year 1000. The various artifacts, found in ruins in northern Greenland, are Norse. They indicate that Norsemen and Eskimos traded extensively, and such cultural refinements as chessmen suggest long-term settlement.

ARTIFACTS: NATIONAL MUSEUM OF COPENHAGEN

idea that this Norse discovery of America was more than an isolated event, one that led neither to permanent settlement nor to important historical consequences.

This impression of the ephemeral and inconsequential character of the Viking experience in America is about to be challenged in a new book, *Viking America*, by James Robert Enterline, which Doubleday & Company will publish this month. According to Enterline, Norse contact with the American mainland actually accelerated just before the fifteenth century, when recorded European communication with Greenland's Norse settlements is known to have been interrupted. Indeed, that very interruption now appears to have been associated with a dispersal of the Greenland settlers, driven by climatic changes from their farms at Julianehaab and Godthaab into hunting grounds on the American continent. The implications for later historical consequences come from

Chess pieces

Spindle

VIKING AMERICA:
A NEW THEORY

*Was Columbus motivated by Norse discoveries,
concealed over the centuries in misinterpreted maps?*

By GERARD L. ALEXANDER

the fact that maps and other kinds of geographic information about that dispersal evidently were rather widely circulated in southern Europe during the century preceding Columbus. If it can be inferred that Columbus was motivated by such information, then the consequences of the Norse discovery were indeed important.

Despite its title, Enterline's book pursues the subject from the standpoint of the history of ideas and avoids an ethnic or partisan approach. The revisory role of the book begins in its second chapter, which lays the groundwork for controverting most of the standard interpretations of the Icelandic sagas recounting Leif Eiriksson's landfalls. It has hitherto been generally held that Markland (Norse for "woodland"), one of these landfalls, was the forest-covered Labrador coast. But close attention to the context of the sagas describing Markland shows, in case after case, that Markland was not a

land of continuous forest cover, but a land of isolated stands of dwarf trees that could be slashed down by Norse battle hatchets. The information that just such isolated stands of dwarf trees do exist far north of the tree line allows the possibility that Markland was much closer to Leif's starting place near Julianehaab in Greenland. Among other things, this fits in better with how long the sagas say Leif took between landfalls.

Vinland has almost always been interpreted to mean "wine land," a land of wild grapes. Yet a small minority of researchers has held to the idea, at least a century old, that the name Vinland was instead based on an archaic Norse word meaning "pastureland." That minority view has now been newly supported. First of all, the evidence shows that the Greenlanders who named Vinland had no knowledge at all of wine or grapes, being mead and beer drinkers. Second, close reading of the sagas describing Vinland shows

that its harvest was not grapes or vines, but hay for the cattle the explorers carried along on shipboard. Third, besides the Vinland Map announced by Yale University in 1965, there are two other old maps that, though not labelling it Vinland, do show a similarly shaped island in the same relative position. In each case the label, irrespective of the language used, means "pastureland."

The first of these maps actually exists in several versions, all of which were made in the early and middle 1400's in central Europe by the so-called Vienna-Klosterneuberg school of cartographers. On this map the island is labelled *Insula Dicolzi*, freely translated as "island of wild cabbage pastures." Unfortunately, little is known about the background of this map, and the source of the information for this Insula Dicolzi is lost to history. The opposite case occurs in the second map, Gerardus Mercator's famous world map of 1569, which introduced the projection

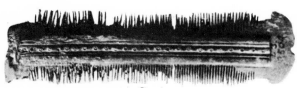

Comb

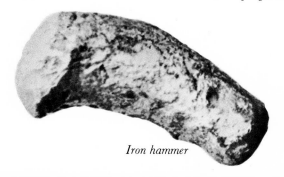

Iron hammer

bearing his name. Mercator's label for the island that the Vinland Map calls Vinland is *Grocland*. Mercator is known to have received this information from Dutch sources two centuries old in 1569, and Grocland in the fourteenth century meant, roughly, "land of wild heather pastures." The source of this Dutch information, in turn, is known to have been very close to the anonymous author of the famous lost book *Inventio Fortunatae*, who travelled throughout all the Norse countries including Greenland in the 1360's, and may well have been escorted on a visit to Vinland.

Acceptance of the meaning "pastureland" for Vinland allows a reinterpretation of its location independently of the northern growth limit of wild grapes. This limit has played an important part in the familiar attempts to identify Vinland as one of various places along the eastern seaboard of the United States. But the speed the Norsemen would have had to attain to reach these places within the sailing times specified by the sagas strains modern credulity as much as it would have strained the Norse ships, and it allows no time for them to have done any exploring along the way. On these grounds Enterline rejects any possibility that Vinland was in Virginia, Massachusetts, or even Maine. The site generally admitted to be Norse at L'Anse-aux-Meadows, Newfoundland, excavated in the 1960's by Helge and Anne Stine Ingstad, lies beyond the northern growth limit of wild grapes but is still a thousand miles southward from Leif's first stopping place, Helluland, generally presumed to be Baffin Island. Furthermore, Enterline demonstrates that the topographic descriptions of Vinland in the sagas are inconsistent with the features of the Newfoundland site. He suggests that while it cannot be Leif's Vinland, L'Anse-aux-Meadows

may well be the remains of Hvitramannaland, another land described in Norse sagas.

Mr. Enterline settles on the location of Leif's Vinland at the very northernmost part of the Quebec-Labrador peninsula, on the west coast of Ungava Bay. Here, he shows, there is an abundance of wild pastures that fulfill the revised interpretation of Vinland. Most important, he gives an analysis of the sagas' geographic descriptions so closely correlated with this Ungava Bay locale that every environmental detail mentioned by the sagas is identifiable with a real feature. No writer arguing in favor of any other identification of Vinland has ever attempted so thorough an analysis. Moreover, unexpectedly and unknown to either party, while he was working out this analysis Canadian researchers were investigating ruins on this very shore on the west of Ungava Bay. They turned out to be Norse.

These results form the foundation of an objective reassessment of Norse history that indicates a much more gradual exploration southward from Greenland than heretofore imagined. And such a reassessment gets strong support from another unexpected source: Eskimo archaeology. The first generations of Norsemen to settle in Greenland found the land uninhabited, and Danish archaeologists have shown that the Eskimos did not arrive until the thirteenth century, at the conclusion of the Thule Eskimo migration eastward across Canada. This Eskimo culture was influenced in many respects by contacts with the Norse culture, and the new hybrid that resulted is known as the Inugsuk culture. Its borrowed features include knowledge of how to make staved barrels and tubs, how to carve saw blades in bone, and how to fashion blades with metal procured from the Norsemen. Enterline sees the locations of Inugsuk Eskimo ruins as a kind of road map of where

the Norsemen had been. These locations suggest that any interest the Norsemen might have had in southward exploration was at least equalled by their interest in northward exploration: there are Inugsuk sites all the way to the northwesternmost corner of Greenland. At this location there have also been found pieces of Norse woven cloth, chain-mail armor, and carved chess pieces. But here the Danish archaeological province ends, and the Canadian record begins.

That record has been investigated less intensively than one might hope, but Enterline has nevertheless collected a number of clues that suggest a most startling conclusion: that the Norsemen had discovered the Northwest Passage. Archaeological and anthropological traces along this route as far west as Alaska are taken by him as hints of an answer to a long-standing question: What were the circumstances under which the Norse settlements in Greenland eventually and mysteriously disappeared? His answer is that when a known climatic deterioration in the late Middle Ages made their already marginal dairy farming no longer possible, the Norsemen had to move to hunting grounds in arctic Canada. The huge herds of arctic caribou, which even now migrate in reduced numbers north and south across the Northwest Passage twice each year, were made up of the most easily killed of all large game animals and evidently provided a relatively comfortable livelihood. In the central Arctic the Norsemen apparently came under Eskimo influence to the same extent as the latter had come under Norse influence in Greenland. These nomadic Norsemen learned the obvious practicality of Eskimo clothing and house-building methods but also the less obviously practical art of making maps. While the earliest known Eskimo culture included the art of communicating geographic information by tracing maps on snow, sand, or driftwood, the Norse-

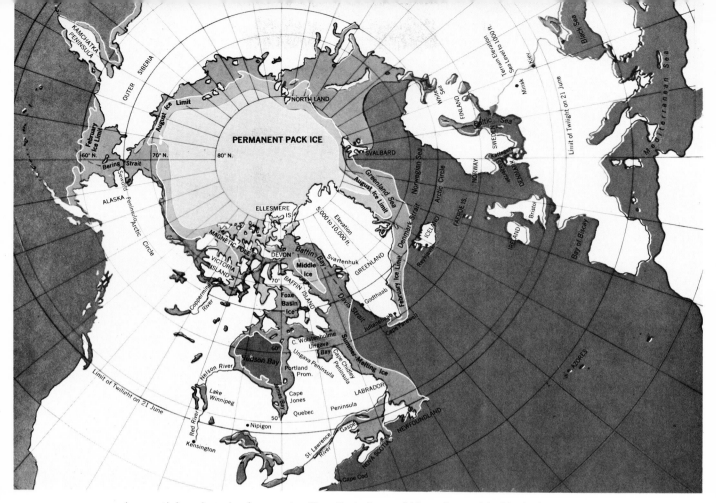

An essential reorientation for grasping Enterline's theory of Norse dispersal in North America is to view the world from the top instead of the usual way. This makes it possible to see why, as they moved westward across the Arctic Archipelago, the Vikings imagined they were in Siberia.

U.S. AIR FORCE

men originally had no tradition whatsoever of map making. This little item of cross-cultural influence was later to have profound results in Europe.

Evidence of Norse explorations southward from Greenland has long been known but is highly controversial. Among the somewhat less controversial evidence is the history of the game lacrosse. Modern man first learned this game from Indians native to the St. Lawrence Valley, but they in turn apparently learned it from the Norsemen. The Norse and Indian versions of the game both contain a feature so unusual—paired opponents whom other teammates may not help or hinder—as to make the probability of independent origin vanishingly small. The other evidence for southward exploration from

Greenland is more controversial. Part of the reason for the controversy has been that some of that evidence, such as the Kensington (Minnesota) "rune stone," indicates a late date (1362) and an interior location inconsistent with the preconception that Norse explorations of Temperate Zone America must have radiated from an eastern-seaboard Vinland. Without insisting on any one of these controversial items as evidence for his theories, Enterline argues that nevertheless they all fall within the pattern of his theory of a late-fourteenth-century dispersal westward from Greenland in subarctic regions, followed by exploration southward from there in the early fifteenth century. But just as this exploration of the temperate part of America was getting under way, officially recog-

nized communication between Europe and Greenland was terminated, presumably because the Norse colonies had ceased to exist. It was never re-established.

The author's picture of the last living Norseman on the North American continent is quite different from the traditional romantic image of some embattled hero in the Greenland settlements in the early fifteenth century succumbing to an Eskimo onslaught. Instead, Enterline's last Norseman is a close friend of the natives in either arctic Canada or the Great Lakes region, having all his cousins of mixed racial stock and finding nobody purely of his own race to marry. It is perhaps the seventeenth century, and he remembers only dimly the language his grandparents used to speak and their

CONTINUED ON PAGE 106

-VI- MEN OF THE REVOLUTION

To read Thomas Jones's acerb *History of New York during the Revolutionary War* is to behold the outward man of the portrait—prim, carping, easily outraged, a nob who looks as though he had sniffed something odious. When he began writing this record in 1783, Judge Jones was prepared to particularize his hates. He was less concerned by then with issues than with people, and he divided his cast of characters into two simple categories: good and bad. Considering the authorship, it is not surprising that the book brims with bile or that rebel sympathizers are represented (to use a few of his phrases) as enemies to monarchy, haters of episcopacy, libellous dissenters, a seditious and rebellious multitude, or simply rabble. Yet Jones was impartial: he had spleen to spare for a legion of bunglers on the other side.

What could one expect, he asked, from a general like Sir Henry Clinton, who was "possessed of so little resolution, such indecision, and such rank timidity" that he was "laughed at by the rebels, despised by the British, and cursed by the loyalists"? Or from Howe, "lolling in the arms of his mistress, and sporting his cash at the faro bank"? As for the British command as a whole, "a fatality, a kind of absurdity, or rather stupidity" had characterized every action they took during the war.

From the time Thomas Jones was born in 1731, he had known the social position and affluence of the fortunate early comer: his grandfather Jones acquired six thousand acres around South Oyster Bay from the Indians, built Long Island's first brick house at Fort Neck, and was granted the highly lucrative monopoly of whaling and other fisheries off Long Island by the Crown. On the old man's tombstone was an inscription he had written himself, ending with these hopeful lines:

Long May his Sons this Peaceful Spot Injoy,
And no Ill Fate his Offspring here Annoy.

Thomas' mother's people arrived in Plymouth, Massachusetts, in 1632 and prospered; his father became speaker of the New York assembly and a justice of the supreme court; and after graduating from Yale in 1750 the son followed him into the law in a manner that smacked of nepotism to Liberty Boys. He married a daughter of James de Lancey, chief justice and lieutenant governor of the province, and in 1773 succeeded his aging father on the bench.

The society to whose orderly maintenance he directed his efforts counted itself civilized—a term implying tranquillity and an absence of savagery. But civilization is a fragile condition: let one element of a community get out of hand and the entire structure may be threatened, as by the furtive onset of a plague. The tradesman encountered on the street last week, all subservience and smiles, wears the face of hate today, and one walks faster, avoiding his eyes and the possibility of contamination. Suddenly the world is all haves and have-nots, each acutely conscious of the other's personal balance sheet. Fear is the handmaiden of daily life, and people listen for the sound in the night that means the barbarian is at the gate . . . as the judge and members of his family could testify.

In June, 1776, while the rebel army occupied New York, the provincial assembly had the judge arrested for failing to answer a summons that required him to prove why he "should be considered a friend of the American cause." He was released on parole, but the warning was clear: something of the sort would occur again. On August 11, with the British threatening to invade Long Island or New York momentarily, Jones was taken into custody and sent for safekeeping to Connecticut, without being charged. Then he was released on parole again. For three anxious years he remained at Fort Neck, theoretically within the protective sphere of the British army but in fact in the no man's land that existed just outside occupied Manhattan. Then it happened: like a gang of latter-day storm troopers a party of militiamen from Fairfield, Connecticut, broke into his home, disregarded his parole, and abducted him in front of family and guests. After ransacking the house, they took him off to Newfield (now Bridgeport), where he was held for the rest of the winter. It seems they wanted someone of suitable rank to exchange for the militia general Gold Selleck Silliman, a Yale classmate and friend, who had been captured by loyalists.

The terror had struck close to home before then, in 1777. Jones's niece Elizabeth Floyd was visiting the daughter of the loyalist Oliver de Lancey at his house on upper Manhattan when they heard voices on the grounds and called from a window, "Who is there?" Instantly the house was broken into by rebel soldiers, who struck the women with muskets and began setting the place on fire. As the ladies ran off in their nightdresses Miss Floyd barely escaped being incinerated when a man threw a burning window curtain over her; Miss de Lancey managed to snatch up her brother's baby from the nursery, and the refugees spent the night in a nearby swamp. Mrs. de Lancey, who was too feeble to run away, hid in a stone dog kennel, from which sanctuary she watched the night raiders burn down her home.

*I*n March, 1781, the judge and his wife, accompanied by Miss Floyd and two servants, sailed for England. His health had deteriorated in prison, and he thought the treatments at Bath might help his rheumatism. He would return, he told friends, as soon as possible. But the end of the war, which he thought would bring peace, brought him no such thing. New York had passed an Act of Attainder, whereby a list of persons charged with "adhering to the enemies of the State" would forfeit not only their property but their lives if they were caught. Thomas Jones was one of those named, and he prudently remained an exile in England until his death in 1792. Before he died, the government to which he had been loyal awarded him £5,447 in compensation, but the sum bore no relationship to the value of what he had lost—two large houses, a huge estate on Long Island, land in New York City and in Westchester, Ulster, Orange, and Tryon counties.

From the judge's standpoint, the accounting could scarcely be reckoned in pounds, shillings, and pence. He had lost what he valued above all else—his country.
—*Richard M. Ketchum*

A FAMOUS HISTORIAN RECALLS THE COUNTRY WHERE HE GREW UP

A Michigan Boyhood

By BRUCE CATTON

We lived in Indian summer and mistook it for spring. Winter lay ahead just when we thought June was on the way. The school, the town, and the people connected with both were coming to an end that seemed to be a beginning. They had been created by an era that was closing, and nothing like them would ever exist again because what had brought them forth was gone; yet twilight at the end of the day looks much as it does at the dawn unless you watch the shadows move, and for a little while time stood still. The shadows were not coming down the slope. They would dissolve when the sun rose, and the future—when it appeared: there was no hurry about it—would wear a familiar image. What we were going to be was determined by what had gone before. We accepted the unbreakable continuity of the society that had produced us.

That continuity, although we did not realize it, was already breaking apart. We knew of course that changes were taking place. The forests were gone, and all around us the little towns were falling into a long decline. The farms that had appeared so hopefully on the hills and in the wide flat valleys were going the same way. One by one—indeed, ten by ten, if anyone had bothered to count—they were going back to brambles and sumac. The section that had found it worthwhile to support us was becoming less and less able to carry the load. School and town had been built to provide a light in the wilderness, but now the wilderness was gone. We understood that there would have to be some readjustments.

But we hardly doubted that the readjustments would

be made. Much had been invested, worth nothing at a sheriff's sale, worth everything to the investors: hard work, sacrifice, courage, and the wavering dreams that make a barren life tolerable because they reach out to something better beyond the high ground ahead. It was not possible that all of these could be wasted. Somehow, someway, all that had been done would justify itself. The light that had been lit on our hilltop could not be allowed to go out just because the surrounding darkness was gone. It would still be needed to light a path for the feet of men not yet taught to lift their eyes to the sky. We never bothered to formulate this faith. We just had it.

It was easy to feel this way because Benzonia's concerns were small—small enough to fit into the deepest recesses of the human heart—and its history was uneventful. The individual might have his own pack of grief, suffering, and shattered hopes to carry as he clambered up the long stairway, but the community as a whole knew contentment. A less worried place probably did not exist anywhere. We were isolated from the rest of the world, and the isolation was pleasant. The happenings that tug at the memory today were small happenings.

The town was essentially a crossroads settlement, with a cluster of wooden business buildings rising where the north-south road intersected the main road from west to east. There were three general stores, a meat market, a bank, a barbershop, a post office, a drugstore, and a blacksmith shop, and for a time there was a run-down hotel that hardly ever had any guests.

On a late summer afternoon our author walks down the long driveway leading from his home above Crystal Lake.

33

The blacksmith shop was interesting, although the blacksmith did not like to have small boys hanging around. He was important to us, however, because if we found any bits of old iron he would buy them from us, and so he was an occasional source of pennies; we had no pocket money whatever, and to get two or three cents was to become rich. Money thus obtained was almost always spent on candy at Simon McDonald's general store. We felt that Mr. McDonald gave more for a penny than the other stores did, and he sold an odd confection of peanut butter coated with chocolate that came three for a penny and was highly enjoyed. This store, by the way, was like the country store of tradition. Toward the rear there was an open space in front of the counter, with a wood-burning stove surrounded by chairs where men sat and smoked corncob pipes and discussed matters of state; I believe there was even a cracker barrel in connection.

Mr. McDonald, a remarkably genial, easygoing man, enjoyed the distinction of being just about the only Democrat in town. Ours was a devoutly Republican community, and when the village went for Theodore Roosevelt in the 1912 election it felt mildly guilty about it. During the 1912 campaign all of us boys wore party campaign buttons pinned to our shirts, and the only Woodrow Wilson buttons I remember seeing were those worn by Mr. McDonald's two sons, Douglas and Dwight. They lived just across the road from us, and we were very good friends, and I used to tease them about those buttons: why wear the emblems of a sure loser? They got even, with accrued interest, when the election returns came in; and sometime next spring Mr. McDonald was duly appointed Benzonia's postmaster. Everybody agreed that this was no more than right; Mr. McDonald was universally liked, and the political spoils system was accepted without question.

North of the business district, if that is the name for it, were the academy grounds, and on all sides there were little roads and lanes lined with residences. Residential lots tended to be large, most of them had their own vegetable gardens, and in a good many cases there was a small barn behind the house; not a barn as a farmer would understand the term, but a sort of shed big enough to shelter a horse or a cow, with room for a buggy, a tiny loft for hay, and a storeroom for harness, gardening tools, and odds and ends of equipment that were just a little too good to throw away. The gardens were important. We always had one, even when we lived in one of the academy buildings, and in summer our evening meal usually consisted of sweet corn and ripe tomatoes, with perhaps some applesauce and cake for dessert. I don't think I have ever tasted anything better in my life.

Corn and tomatoes taken from the garden less than an hour before they appeared on the table had a flavor that today's city dweller cannot even imagine.

For several years we kept a cow, quartering it in somebody's back-yard barn in the village and taking it out to pasture in a lot on the edge of town. To Robert, and then to me, fell the task of caring for this beast, and it was a task I did not enjoy. I did not so much mind the actual milking, but leading the cow off to pasture in the morning, collecting it in the evening, and going through the ritual of cleaning the stable, getting hay in the manger, spreading straw for bedding, and hoisting buckets of water for the cow to drink did not appeal to me in the least. I do recall one morning when I was taking this creature down a remote lane to its pasture. I had seen, somewhere, an improbable picture of a rosy-cheeked Dutch girl tending a cow, and she had posed prettily with one arm around the cow's neck; it had looked most picturesque, and so—nobody being anywhere about—I thought I would try it myself. The result was not good. My coat was covered with fine hairs, I smelled of cow all day long, and the beast stepped on my foot. We were on a lane that was ankle-deep in soft sand, or I would have had some broken bones. I never again tried to pose with a cow, and to this day I approve of cows only at a distance. It occurs to me that some of my worst moments have come when I was trying to strike an attitude.

One of the pleasantest holidays of the year was Memorial Day, universally known then as Decoration Day because it was the day when you went out to the cemetery and decorated graves. This day of course belonged to the Civil War veterans, although as years passed it more and more became a day to put flowers on the grave of any loved one who had died, and when it came just about everyone in town went to the cemetery with a basket of lilacs. Lilacs grow like weeds in our part of the country, and most farmers planted a long row of lilacs as windbreaks around their houses; in town almost every house had lilacs in the yard, and in late May the scent of them lay on the breeze. To this day I never see lilac blossoms without remembering those Decoration Day observances of long ago.

The Civil War veterans were men set apart. On formal occasions they wore blue uniforms with brass buttons and black campaign hats, by the time I knew them most of them had long gray beards, and whatever they may have been as young men they had an unassuming natural dignity in old age. They were pillars, not so much of the church (although most of them were devout communicants) as of the community; the keepers of its patriotic traditions, the living embodiment, so to speak, of what it most deeply believed about the nation's greatness and high destiny.

They gave an especial flavor to the life of the village.

The senior class of Benzonia Academy, 1916. Bruce Catton is the young man at far right; the girl in the dark suit, front row, is the one with whom he violated Miss Ellis' instructions when the final curtain came down on the commencement play.

AUTHOR'S COLLECTION

Years ago they had marched thousands of miles to legendary battlefields, and although they had lived half a century since then in our quiet backwater all anyone ever thought of was that they had once gone to the ends of the earth and seen beyond the farthest horizon. There was something faintly pathetic about these lonely old men who lived so completely in the past that they had come to see the war of their youth as a kind of lost golden age, but as small boys we never saw the pathos. We looked at these men in blue, existing in pensioned security, honored and respected by all, moving past the mounded graves with their little flags and their heaps of lilacs, and we were in awe of them. Those terrible names out of the history books—Gettysburg, Shiloh, Stone's River, Cold Harbor—came alive through these men. They had *been* there . . . and now they stood by the little G.A.R. monument in the cemetery and listened to the orations and the prayers and the patriotic songs, and to watch them was to be deeply moved.

In their final years the G.A.R. men quietly faded away. Their story had been told and retold, affectionate tolerance was beginning to take the place of respectful awe, and in Europe there was a new war that by its sheer incomprehensible magnitude seemed to dwarf that earlier war we knew so well. One by one the old men went up to that sun-swept hilltop to sleep beneath the lilacs, and as they departed we began to lose more than we knew we were losing. For these old soldiers, simply by existing, had unfailingly expressed the faith we lived by; not merely a faith learned in church, but something that shaped us as we grew up. We could hardly have put it into words, and it would not have occurred to us to try, but we oriented our lives to it and if disorientation lay ahead of us it would come very hard. It was a faith in the continuity of human experience, in the progress of the nation toward an ideal, in the ability of men to come triumphantly through any challenge. That faith lived, and we lived by it.

The school year began late in September, and it always seemed to me that then the town came to life. The youngsters returned from the distant outside world, and our own world was complete again. There were old

CONTINUED ON PAGE 98

LOCAL HISTORY MAKES GOOD—SOMETIMES

Above is one of several rooms in the state capitol in Madison occupied by the State Historical Society of Wisconsin from 1866 to 1900. Twenty years before that, its archives had rested first in a church basement, then reputedly in a bookcase in the governor's office.

The systematic collection of the sources of local, as well as of national, history began in the United States with the organization in 1791 of the Massachusetts Historical Society. This small body, composed of clergymen, lawyers, physicians, and what used to be called merchants (now known as businessmen), undertook the preservation of books, manuscripts, and records that would conduce "to mark the genius, delineate the manners, and trace the progress of society in the United States." They were fully aware that such sources must be collected before they could be preserved. This they undertook energetically, guided by this statement made by the Reverend Jeremy Belknap, the founder, in a letter of February 19, 1791, to Ebenezer Hazard:

By WALTER MUIR WHITEHILL

We intend to be an *active*, not a *passive*, literary body; not to be waiting, like a bed of oysters, for the tide (of communication) to flow in upon us, but to *seek* and *find*, to *preserve* and *communicate*, literary intelligence, especially in the historical way.

The pattern established in Boston was so widely emulated that by the outbreak of the Civil War more than sixty similar societies had been started. The New-York Historical Society was founded in 1804; the American Antiquarian Society in Worcester, Massachusetts, in 1812. Along the Atlantic seaboard, privately supported historical societies that have survived to the present were organized in Maine, Rhode Island, New Hampshire, and Pennsylvania in the 1820's; in Virginia, Vermont, Connecticut, and Georgia in the 1830's; in Maryland and New Jersey in the 1840's; in South Carolina in the 1850's. By 1860 every state east of Texas, with the single exception of Delaware, had such a society; in 1859 United States Army officers even organized one in the territory of New Mexico.

On the frontier, historical societies were founded early, sometimes before there was any substantial body of history to record. In 1849, less than eight months after the establishment of Minnesota Territory, when most of the area was still occupied by Indians, the fifth act of the territorial legislature was the incorporation of a Minnesota Historical Society. This cheerful anachronism, comparable to the notion of establishing historical societies at Jamestown in 1607 or at Plymouth in 1620, occurred at a time when the five thousand white inhabitants of Minnesota were confined to a small wedge between the St. Croix and Mississippi rivers. In such frontier regions support had to come from the state through legislative appropriation. In the older cities, where prosperity permitted some leisure for literary and historical pursuits, historical societies continued to

depend upon voluntary support.

Not all the organizations that were so hopefully founded accomplished anything or even long survived. Those that did owed their success to devoted individuals like the Boston clergyman Jeremy Belknap, the New York merchant John Pintard, or the scholar-printer Isaiah Thomas, who were the founders, respectively, of the Massachusetts and the New-York historical societies and the American Antiquarian Society. When the New Jersey Historical Society was being founded in 1845, the Reverend Samuel Miller offered the new organization a piece of advice, based on experience with the New-York Historical Society, which he had helped John Pintard to found forty-

The first home of the Massachusetts Historical Society was in the library room of the Massachusetts Bank of Boston.

one years earlier. "I have observed," he wrote, "in regard to all the literary and scientific societies with which I have ever been connected, that, however numerous the members, some dozen or two of them performed all the work." It should be noted that these workers were chiefly professional men or merchants, not usually associated with academic institutions, for, until the foundation of the American Historical Association in 1884, universities and colleges concerned themselves relatively little with American history. Where there were devoted amateurs or local antiquaries who were willing to work, historical societies flourished; where

they were in short supply, or lazy, such organizations foundered. The inglorious career of the Historical Society of Mississippi will serve as an example. Not long after its foundation in 1858 it was discovered that only three members had paid the very reasonable dues of one dollar; the society therefore gave up the ghost in discouragement.

But the older historical societies that have lasted, for periods ranging from one hundred to 181 years, have, as their chief excuse for existence, collected, preserved, made available to scholars, and published source materials of American history. They have done so, without fanfare, from private funds that are astonishingly small for the results achieved. Until the last quarter of the nineteenth century, these old eastern state historical societies carried on virtually unaided the work of preserving sources and making them available. In the twentieth century other organizations became concerned with American history—private and university libraries, federal and state archival agencies, historical museums and restorations. Yet these newer allies have not supplanted the older historical societies, as one will readily see by examining current historical literature. Few books of American history are published today without some expression of the author's gratitude to one of the older societies for assistance or for permission to publish manuscripts in their possession.

The library of the Massachusetts Historical Society is locally oriented, for it specializes in basic printed materials relating to Massachusetts and, in a broader sense, to New England. Its manuscript collection has a far wider scope, and, being second only to that of the Library of Congress, it is an essential source for national as well as local history. It is, moreover, quite as concerned with the present as with earlier centuries. A 1968 pamphlet, *American History and the*

Massachusetts Historical Society, contains this significant paragraph:

It is an unfortunate but not uncommon error to suppose that historical societies, this one included, are concerned only with the quaint and antique and distant past, just as schoolchildren (and too many of their parents and teachers) suppose that history is something in costume and ended soon after 1800, or at the latest at Appomattox Court House. No one at the Massachusetts Historical Society wears a powdered wig, and today in its storage areas the sources for recent history compete for shrinking shelf room with colonial diaries and whalers' logs. Modern files of papers tend to be bulkier than older ones; the recent gift of Senator Leverett Saltonstall's [U.S. Senator from Massachusetts, 1944–67] papers, for example, weighed seven tons as delivered from Washington in General Service Administration trucks. The Society's Director estimated in 1967 that the physical bulk of our manuscript acquisitions had *quadrupled* since the Second World War.

Although the Massachusetts Historical Society is supported, as it has been since 1791, by a rigidly limited body of semihonorary members, its resources are freely available to any qualified scholar, irrespective of membership. And through its numerous publications they are in part available to people who never set foot in Boston. The society has published more than 250 volumes in letterpress—*Collections*, *Proceedings*, and special series; it pioneered fifty-five years ago with a series of *Photostat Americana*, by which hundreds of rare pamphlets, runs of early newspapers, and certain rare books and manuscripts were duplicated for subscribing libraries. It has more recently, in cooperation with the National Historical Publications Commission, published a number of important groups of manuscripts on microfilm, as well as editing, for let-terpress publication by the Belknap Press of Harvard University Press, numerous volumes of *The Adams Papers*.

Other of the older historical societies have, in addition to maintaining important libraries and manuscript collections, made their resources available not only through books but through quarterly journals. *The Pennsylvania Magazine of History and Biography* has been published since 1877 by the Historical Society of Pennsylvania; the *Virginia Magazine of History and Biography* since 1893 by the Virginia Historical Society; while the *New-York Historical Society Quarterly* has appeared regularly since 1917. The American Antiquarian Society, whose interests once somewhat resembled those of the Society of Antiquaries of London, has become today a national library of American history, specializing in American imprints and in newspaper collections. One of its remarkable contributions to learning is *Early American Imprints*, edited by Clifford K. Shipton, which is a microprint edition of every extant book, pamphlet, and broadside printed in what is now the United States from 1639 to the end of the year 1800.

While these and a number of the other old, privately supported state historical societies have deliberately focused their activities upon efforts to assist serious scholars, many of the publicly supported societies, particularly in the Mississippi Valley, have also been concerned with the popularization of local history among the residents of their states. The State Historical Society of Wisconsin, for example, has long combined scholarly activities with an aggressive program of what it likes to call "taking history to the people." Thus in addition to publishing serious biographies and historical monographs and such valuable works of reference as *Guide to Wisconsin Newspapers, 1833–1957*, and a *Dictionary of Wisconsin Biography*, it issues such juve-nile titles as *A Merry Briton in Pioneer Wisconsin; It Happened Here; Stories of Wisconsin;* and *Side Roads: Excursions into Wisconsin's Past*, in which "one of Wisconsin's favorite story-tellers," Fred Holmes, "spins tales of nostalgia about his native state's ice cream parlors, barbershops, country stores, German beer gardens, and Christmas customs at the turn of the century." This nostalgic aspect of the not very distant past is also often emphasized in the society's museum in Madison by the display of a Model T Ford, barbershop mugs, the reconstruction of a drugstore, or other objects certain to give any citizen of Wisconsin who happens in a pleasing shock of recognition. The society maintains various sites and buildings throughout the state, including a stagecoach inn at Greenbush, a farm and craft museum at Cassville, and the Circus World Museum at Baraboo. At the latter, elephant rides, cotton candy, pink lemonade are to be had, and, among other delights offered by the society's flyer:

You can have yourself photographed in a cage with a living, roaring, black-maned African lion assuring yourself and your children a triumph of indescribable sensations and novel photographs.

And all without risk, for these modern Daniels are well protected by invisible glass from the living, roaring animal into whose cage, for a consideration, they are permitted to enter. The society further encourages children to become "junior historians" —a phrase I find as irritating as the euphemistic "senior citizens," so often applied today in the United States to anyone over sixty-five. Operation on so many levels is, of course, only possible in an institution liberally supported by public grants, for much of the appeal "to a wide audience never before exposed to the society or to history" is, consciously or otherwise, a confirmation of a remark made in 1909 by Reuben Gold

Thwaites (the distinguished head of the State Historical Society of Wisconsin from 1887 to 1913) that "legislatures and the public at large that they represent require coddling if their support is to be obtained."

While the state historical societies, whether publicly or privately supported, often contain resources of national as well as local interest, there is a multitude of purely local ones. Although in recent years certain of the larger publicly supported state historical societies, of which Minnesota is the most conspicuous example, have systematically inspired the organization of county counterparts which receive some assistance from taxes, the greater part of local historical societies owe their origin to the interest and devotion of people on the spot who genuinely care for the characteristics of their region. Some go back into the nineteenth century, but the greater part are of twentieth-century foundation.

My own Massachusetts county has its society, the Essex Institute in Salem, organized in 1848 through the amalgamation of societies going back to 1821 and 1833. Among county societies in the United States, it unquestionably takes first place for the extent and richness of its library and manuscripts and its century-long record of continuous scholarly publication. One might think that the Essex Institute would, by itself, be able to minister to all the historical needs of the immediate region, for Essex is not a large county. It contains 355,840 acres. After deducting tidal marsh, ponds, rivers, and swamps, it has only 299,551 acres useful for tillage, woodlands, and the sites of its thirty-four cities and towns. But this small area has, for the United States, a long and varied history, for its settlement goes back to the 1620's. It has, in addition, a preoccupation with history that is out of all proportion to its size, for twenty-seven out of its thirty-four cities and towns have local societies

of their own. Thus Essex County has a historical society for every 10,660 acres of dry land, which must constitute some sort of a record, even for a country of "joiners." Some have worthwhile collections, adequate financial support, competent professional staff that justify their existence. Others, at least in my jaundiced view, are centers of nostalgia, serving chiefly as insecure and leaky bastions against change, and scarcely would be missed.

This is far from all, when one considers the specialized activities of the Peabody Museum of Salem (founded in 1799; maritime and natural history), the Robert S. Peabody Foundation for Archaeology (American Indian) and the Addison Gallery of

The New-York Historical Society first met in Old City Hall, formerly Federal Hall, where Washington was inaugurated.

American Art at Phillips Academy, Andover, the Merrimack Valley Textile Museum in North Andover, and the reconstruction of a seventeenth-century ironworks in Saugus, now maintained by the National Park Service. In addition, the Society for the Preservation of New England Antiquities maintains three historic houses each in Ipswich and Newbury, two in Danvers, one each in Gloucester, Rowley, and Saugus, and the Rocky Hill Meeting House of 1785 in Amesbury. The Trustees of Reservations (which antedate the National Trust in Great Britain) preserve not only great tracts of land but houses in Ipswich and North

Andover, while the birthplace of the poet John Greenleaf Whittier in Haverhill and his home in Amesbury are exhibited by separate charitable corporations organized for that express purpose. Indeed, the multiplicity of historical organizations within this small area reminds me of nothing so much as Augustus de Morgan's inelegant jingle:

> *Great fleas have little fleas upon*
> *their backs to bite 'em,*
> *And little fleas have lesser fleas*
> *and so ad infinitum. . . .*

Essex County, Massachusetts, is an extreme case, but throughout the United States there are more local historical societies than anyone can accurately count. The American Association for State and Local History, founded in 1940 in the hope of tying some of this diffuse activity together, a decade ago sent questionnaires to approximately 1,700 local historical societies across the country. From the replies of the 565 who troubled to answer, as well as from 120 personal visits, Dr. Richmond D. Williams, who conducted this survey, drew various conclusions. Among them was the saddening discovery of a twenty-year "life cycle" for birth and death. Of the 1,343 societies listed in the association's 1944 directory, 502 seemed to have died by the 1961 revision. The answer is not hard to find. Frequently, in New England at least, a single determined lady, who might pull poison ivy from colonial gravestones with her own hands until the town authorities were shamed into taking better care of a seventeenth-century cemetery, would badger her neighbors into the preservation of a local building and thus initiate both a society and a collection. But if she and her coadjutors failed to recruit adequate younger successors, the society might well die with them, leaving a house in poor repair, with a plow, a wing chair, a flax spinning wheel, a luster tea set, somebody's wedding dress, a tin oven, and other objects too good to throw away jumbled together in its rooms.

The restoration of Williamsburg, Virginia, begun in 1927 through the extraordinary generosity of the late John D. Rockefeller, Jr., who before his death in 1960 had given some 68.5 million dollars to the project, produced a unique example of *le temps perdu sous cloche*. As the intention was to turn back the clock and return the town to its appearance as a colonial capital, some six hundred nineteenth- and twentieth-century buildings were eventually torn down or moved outside the restoration area; eighty-five surviving eighteenth-century buildings were restored to their original appearance; while the Capitol, Governor's Palace, and the Raleigh Tavern, which had disappeared, were meticulously reconstructed. Today Williamsburg is a museum piece, an eighteenth-century fantasy in which the more pleasing aspects of colonial life are evoked (with the omission of smells, flies, pigs, dirt, and slave quarters), sheltered from the outside world (figuratively if not literally) by a vast glass case. In her recent *New Lives, New Landscapes*, Nan Fairbrother classified amenity and preservation societies

in three progressive states, as Reversers, Shunters, and Translators. Reversers are simple: they want to put the clock back. They would like us all to live happily in a beautiful pre-industrial world, despite the fact that no one would now tolerate the pre-industrial life.

Williamsburg is the most brilliant and most extensive example in the United States of Reversers at work.

The immense popularity of Williamsburg, which coincided with the widespread proliferation of automobiles, led to the creation after the Second World War of a number of open-air museums, to which old buildings in danger on their original sites were moved. At Cooperstown the New York State Historical Asso-

ciation collected together a school, church, country store, tavern, and small offices to form a "Village Crossroads" as an adjunct to its imaginative and beautifully installed Farmers' Museum. At Mystic, Connecticut, the Marine Historical Association, Inc., assembled ships, smaller craft, and buildings to create a synthetic seaport of the nineteenth century, of equally nostalgic intent. Two other assemblies of old buildings in New England have become institutions from the enthusiastic acquisitiveness of private collectors. Old Sturbridge Village in Sturbridge, Massachusetts, sprang from the antique collecting of Albert B. and J. Cheney Wells of Southbridge; the Shelburne Museum in Vermont from the omnivorous accumulations of the late Mrs. J. Watson Webb. Old Stur-

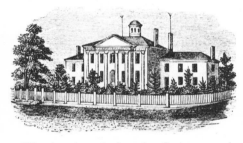

The American Antiquarian Society moved from the home of founder Isaiah Thomas to this building in Worcester in 1820.

bridge Village presents a pleasing illusion of an actual New England community; at Shelburne the impression is simply of a fine field in which buildings from various parts of New England have been reassembled after moving, to house Mrs. Webb's miscellaneous collections. Sometimes it seems that these efforts confuse rather than enhance local history, for although they have rescued from destruction some buildings by moving, their primary purpose is the creation of a well-walled illusion within which the visitor may enjoy a synthetic "past" that relieves

the ugliness and monotony of the tedium in which he spends most of his life. "There is," in addition, as the city planner Carl Feiss has pointed out,

a curious contradiction in the great popularity of the simulated villages used as museums, while real villages, one after the other, are subject to the deterioration and misuse caused by the automobile age. In fact, villages on the way to Sturbridge and several other historic museums, which in their own right had at one time great beauty and artistic value, are being destroyed by those very tourists who are looking for quaintness and culture at the museums. In just the same way that the flower market, the Place Verte in Brussels, has been converted to a parking lot, so have village green after village green in New England.

The instigators of these nostalgic dream images of an immutable past consider their villages legitimate offspring of the open-air folk museums of Scandinavia. It should be remembered, however, that the prototype of these institutions, Skansen in Stockholm, was founded by Artur Hazelius at a moment in the 1880's when Sweden was rapidly being industrialized and numerous artists and writers were consoling themselves by reviving the memory of a simpler agricultural world in which none of these nasty things existed. As Dr. Ingvar Anderson has remarked, "They harked back to a world of fantasy that bore no relation to modern Sweden." . . . According to Nan Fairbrother's definition, the proponents of open-air museums are Shunters, "more realistic but less sympathetic" than Reversers:

They accept that modern living means unattractive developments like cement works and pylons, but propose to shunt them into someone else's territories.

According to her,

The Translators are the most advanced and therefore most useful: they appreciate the past but accept the future, and aim to incorporate the inevitable changes with least harm, and even with benefit, to the environment. Most serious societies (whatever the still-blinkered attitudes of some of their members) are now reaching this advanced stage of realism and responsibility.

This is equally true in the United States. For many decades, whenever anyone succeeded in rescuing a fine old building, the principal use contemplated was to turn it into a museum for the edification and inspiration of visitors. The United States already has on exhibition more historic houses and museums than it needs or can afford or are good for it as a nation. And some of these deal out, in the sacred name of "education," some pretty dubious nostalgia, disguised as "history." But the Translators are now at the helm. *Historic Preservation Tomorrow*, issued by the National Trust for Historic Preservation in 1967, states unequivocally on page 1:

Only in exceptional cases should a historic building be converted to museum use. The objective is to conserve buildings by continuing to use them for their original, or compatible purposes.

Again it is stated that "the emphasis should be on the historic structures and their sites as components of viable neighborhoods." Such an approach gives hope that local history will count buildings, as well as books and manuscripts, among its documents in the future.

During the nineteenth century countless histories of towns were written, especially in New England. In the last third of the century, with the simultaneous (but unrelated) development of the "scientific" study of American history at universities and the ancestor hunting of persons attempting to qualify for membership in newly formed hered-

itary patriotic societies, history and genealogy became estranged. Although it was long the fashion for historians to ignore, or speak patronizingly of, the older town histories, these same books today often prove invaluable sources for social history and demography, since they contain so much specific information about actual people.

Although most recent town histories are chiefly of interest to residents, there are occasional happy exceptions, like Edward Pierce Hamilton's *A History of Milton*, published by the Milton Historical Society in 1957. I could wish that we had had more American equivalents of the late Reginald L. Hine's delightful volumes on every possible aspect of the history of his Hertfordshire town of Hitchin. In Massachusetts a good deal of local history gets written because of the personal enthusiasms of historians who have other strings for their bows. . . . J. Frank Dobie's *Guide to Life and Literature of the Southwest*, first published in 1942 and "revised and enlarged in both knowledge and wisdom" in 1952, contains a passage that is of universal application in regard to local history:

I have heard so much silly bragging by Texans that I now think it would be a blessing to themselves—and a relief to others—if the braggers did not know they lived in Texas. Yet the time is not likely to come when a human being will not be better adapted to his environments by knowing their nature; on the other hand, to study a provincial setting from a provincial point of view is restricting. Nobody should specialize on provincial writings before he has the perspective that only a good deal of good literature and wide history can give. I think it is more important that a dweller in the Southwest read the trial and death of Socrates than all the books extant on killings by Billy the Kid. I think this dweller will fit his land better by understanding Thomas Jefferson's oath ("I have sworn upon the altar of God eternal hostility against every form of tyranny over the mind of man") than by reading

all the books that have been written on ranch life and people. There are no substitutes for nobility, beauty, and wisdom. One of the chief impediments to amplitude and intellectual freedom is provincial inbreeding. I am sorry to see the writings of the Southwest substituted for noble and beautiful and wise literature to which all people everywhere are inheritors.

Local history is admirable when its subject is recognized as a microcosm, as an epitome of the great world. Reginald L. Hine knew this when he spoke of the comfort

which the parish historian needs to hug to his heart. His little corner of the universe, wherein he seems to sit alone whispering to himself, is the universe itself; or as old writers were fond of saying, *speculum mundi*—a little mirror of the world. However the lords of creation may despise him he may hold up his head, for the story of an English town is the story of England itself; and I am not sure whether the spectacle of human life is not more vividly seen refracted through the private experience of a single parish.

When, however, local history becomes an end in itself, a substitute for knowledge of the rest of the world, or a legal requirement in school and college curricula, as is the case in some American states, there is grave danger of its doing harm. Three more sentences of Frank Dobie's, to which Reginald L. Hine would have subscribed had he ever seen them, furnish good guideposts for anyone concerned with local history: "Good writing about any region is good only to the extent that it has universal appeal. Nothing is too trivial for art, but good art treats nothing in a trivial way. Nothing is too provincial for the regional writer, but he cannot be provincial-minded toward it."

Mr. Whitehill is the director and librarian of the noted Boston Athenaeum. This article originally appeared in The Times Literary Supplement *of London.*

MEN, WOMEN, and MARGARET FULLER

By JOSEPH JAY DEISS

Poe's witticism was not meant kindly, but it was actually a compliment. Without doubt Margaret Fuller stood first among women of the nineteenth century. It is surprising that, as America's first liberated female, she is not today first in the hearts of her countrywomen. The primary responsibility for this neglect lies with her intimate friend Ralph Waldo Emerson, who, under the guise of loving kindness, defeminized, distorted, and diminished the image of her that has come down to us.

Though today almost forgotten, Margaret Fuller still probably holds more firsts than any other American woman who ever lived. As editor of the transcendentalist *Dial*, she was the first woman editor of an important intellectual magazine. She was the first woman to write a book about the West and such experiences as sleeping in a barroom, shooting rapids in an Indian canoe, and witnessing maltreatment of the red man by the white man. She was the first woman to break the taboo against the female sex in the Harvard College Library. As columnist for Horace Greeley's New York *Tribune*, she was the first U.S. woman journalist and and the first professional literary critic of either sex in the United States. Her sensational book, *Woman*

in the Nineteenth Century (1845), was the first uncompromising plea by an American woman for women's rights. Encouraged to go to Europe by Greeley, she was the first American woman foreign correspondent. And while covering the bloody Roman Revolution of 1849, she became the first American woman underground revolutionary in a foreign cause.

She was also the one passion blossom in the flowering of New England, as her friends—Emerson, Bronson Alcott, William Henry Channing, James Freeman Clarke, Thoreau, Elizabeth Hoar, the Peabody sisters —and her enemies—Poe, James Russell Lowell, Longfellow, Hawthorne—were to discover with shock. She dared, in the end, to fulfill herself as a woman—to cease being a "strange, lilting, lean old maid," as Thomas Carlyle described her, and take a lover. The secret was kept until her marriage was announced. That her consort was an Italian revolutionary nobleman over a decade younger, the father of her year-old child, was stunning. It proved too much for even the practical, liberal Greeley, and it cost her her job.

Only very recently have new details been published that reveal the true story of Margaret's life abroad, changing markedly the image Emer-

son passed on to posterity after her death. Emerson dominated a triumvirate, with Channing and Clarke, to edit her so-called *Memoirs*. His tricky techniques—whether deliberate or unconscious—converted her from a warm, rich, loving personality into a snobbish, egotistical, passionless old maid.

She was indeed strange and lilting, but for all Carlyle's description of her at thirty-six, not truly "lean." He meant, probably, that she was not so buxom as an English matron. In fact, however, she was a large-breasted woman whose figure had already developed fully by the time she was thirteen. She was able to dance endlessly and to ride a score of miles horseback without fatigue. Everyone admitted that she dressed in the best of taste and carried herself regally. She was a gifted mimic with a wry sense of humor and occasionally a lacerating tongue. Horace Greeley said she might have been "the first actress of the nineteenth century."

The legend that she was "phenomenally homely," as even the distinguished Professor Perry Miller of Harvard wrote in an article in AMERICAN HERITAGE in February, 1957, was based on descriptions by men perhaps jealous of her intellectual achieve-

This portrait by an unknown artist depicts an elegant and vital Margaret Fuller.

ments who apparently wished to de-feminize her. "Those who seem over-laden with electricity frighten those around them," Margaret observed. Emerson, in contrast to his own pulpit voice, found her tones "nasal"; and Channing described her neck, in the tactful Victorian tradition, as swanlike. Less tactfully, he added that it "made swift turns like that of a bird of prey." The strand of tawny blond hair that survives negates all claims that it was stringy and luster-less. Frederic Hedge, her contemporary, declared that she had "blond and abundant hair, excellent teeth, and sparkling, dancing, busy eyes." True, she was nearsighted and squinted disconcertingly.

Though Emerson confessed he was unable to understand why Italian men paid court to her, Europeans found her graceful and charming. The great Polish poet Adam Mickiewicz wrote to her: "After having admired the women of Rome, say to yourself, 'I too am beautiful!' . . . In you I met a *real* person. I need not give you any other praise." Firmly her New England colleagues belittled her appearance. "She had no pretensions to beauty," James Freeman Clarke said. Yet he admitted, "She was not plain." Elizabeth Hoar, that dry New England intellect who described Emerson as a "ray of white light" and Margaret as a "prism," summed up: "Only her presence can give you the meaning of the name Margaret Fuller."

In one of her innumerable candid appraisals of herself, Margaret wrote: "I am 'too fiery' . . . yet I wish to be seen as I am, and would lose all rather than soften away anything." This honesty endured to the end of her life.

Sarah Margaret Fuller was born May 23, 1810, in the village of Cambridgeport, Massachusetts. Margaret's father, Timothy Fuller, had worked his way through Harvard Law School and had been elected to the United States House of Repre-sentatives as a Jeffersonian. The Fullers were descended from one Thomas Fuller, a pious and poetry-writing Englishman who settled in Salem in 1638. Timothy's father, a clergyman, had opposed the signing of the United States Constitution on the grounds that it condoned human slavery. The cantankerous Fullers had a tradition of speaking out when the spirit moved them.

Timothy at the age of thirty married Miss Margarett Crane, a young woman of twenty, sweet and passive but far from unintelligent—as so often has been implied. Margaret was the first of eight children, of whom two died in infancy and the youngest, a boy, developed mental illness. As Timothy had wanted a boy for his first-born, he resolved to educate Margaret exactly as if she might someday be a candidate for all-male Harvard.

Until Margaret was sent away to boarding school, in adolescence, Timothy assigned her lessons and heard her recitations. At the age of four and a half she could read, and by six was reading Latin with the fluency of English. From Latin she went on to Italian, French, German, a smattering of Greek—studying the masters in each language. She became so versatile that schoolmates invented the legend that she could simultaneously eat an apple, rock a cradle, knit a stocking, and read a book. They were not far wrong.

For this energetic precocity Margaret paid a price: she was set apart from her schoolgirl companions, and boys her own age were bewildered by her. It is hardly surprising that as a child she walked in her sleep and had nightmares of colossal faces and rampant stallions. At eight she read and was deeply affected by *Romeo and Juliet*. Much later she wrote, "At eight or nine years old the passions are not infrequently felt in their full shock." Her appraisal of her childhood was succinct: "The child fed with meat instead of milk becomes too soon matured. . . ."

When Margaret was twenty-three, her father, after a series of economic reverses, dragged the family to a rocky, isolated farm in Groton, Massachusetts. For Margaret it was a period of exile and despair, unrelieved by outside social and intellectual contacts. On Timothy's sudden death two years later, Margaret gave up her dream of Europe and assumed the responsibility for supporting the family. This she did by teaching school in Providence and later by her Boston "Conversations." These were lectures for women on such subjects as Greek mythology and religion, and, despite ridicule, they established her reputation among the local intellectuals.

It was in this period, about 1835, that she first met Emerson. She was twenty-five, he thirty-two. Then began, in Emerson's words, that "strange, cold-warm, attractive-repelling" relationship that was to endure with many temperature variations for the remainder of her life.

Given the time and place of Margaret's birth, her education, and her ecstatic nature, it was perhaps inevitable that she should gravitate toward the transcendentalist camp. Yet she never subscribed fully to transcendentalist ambiguities and finally broke with the movement. She held reservations about so exciting a project as George Ripley's Brook Farm experiment in communal living. The Transcendentalist Club split over the issue, with Emerson exclaiming sententiously, "I am not bitten by this madness of Socialism." While Margaret, on the other hand, called herself an "ardent Socialist," she felt that Brook Farm was not so much socialistic as idealistic. She did not join the commune but often visited to lead classes.

When the transcendentalist group, after much debate, decided in 1840 to establish a journal, the *Dial*, Margaret was chosen editor. This post she held for two years; she was succeeded by Emerson. It was in the pages of the *Dial* that Margaret launched her one-woman campaign for women's rights. Once in her journal she had written, " 'Tis an evil lot to have a man's ambition and a woman's heart." In 1843 she published an article with the ungainly title "The Great Lawsuit—Man *versus* Men: Woman *versus* Women," on the theme that she later developed more fully in her book on women's rights. It aroused controversy in a small circle—not enough, however, to satisfy Margaret.

Then she went West, completed and published her travel book, *Summer on the Lakes*, and—with a pause only long enough to refill her inkwell—resumed her discussion of women's rights. Writing at frantic pace—and as usual not bothering to parse or prune her sentences—she produced *Woman in the Nineteenth Century*, published in New York in February of 1845. Now, she wrote triumphantly, "the measure of my footprint would be left on the earth." The immediate result was as if she had been wearing hobnail boots.

The polite and well-bred were truly horrified at Miss Fuller's brazenness. The book was met with jeers, derision, mockery. It was denounced as preposterous, hysterical, immoral. The first edition was sold out within a week. It became known abroad. "Margaret Fuller" was soon a household name—inspiring to some and revolting to others.

The book was filled with a series of shockers:

"There exists in the minds of men a tone of feeling toward women as toward slaves."

"What Woman needs is not as a woman to act or rule, but as a nature to grow, as an intellect to discern, as a soul to live freely and unimpeded."

"[Men] think that nothing is so much to be dreaded for a woman as originality of thought or character."

"Let it not be said, wherever there is energy or creative genius, 'She has a masculine mind.' "

"Were [women] free, were they able fully to develop the strength and beauty of Woman, they would never wish to be men or manlike."

"There is no wholly masculine man, no purely feminine woman."

"Women are the best helpers of one another. Let them think, let them act."

"We would have every arbitrary barrier thrown down. We would have every path laid open to Woman as freely as to Man."

Horace Greeley, whose publishing firm had accepted *Woman*, had shrewdly foreseen the response. Already he had invited Margaret to come to New York as the first female member of the working press. Though he carped about Margaret's statement that women should be sea captains if they wished, and refused to open doors for her, he gave her free rein. Her articles were to alternate between social and literary criticism. Since Boston intellectuals regarded New York as an uncultured, materialistic Babylon, the fact that Margaret—ignoring clucks from Emerson—accepted the job was considered little short of treason. She began work in December of 1844, soon scandalizing everyone by interviewing prostitutes in Sing Sing prison.

Margaret's treason was magnified when she reviewed scathingly the works of New Englanders Longfellow and Lowell and dissected Emerson's second series of essays and his poems as if working on a cadaver. She did not hesitate to be scalpel precise about Emerson: "We miss what we expect in the work of the great poet or the great philosopher," she wrote about the essays. "Here is undoubtedly the man of ideas, but we want the ideal man also; want the heart and genius of human life to interpret it, and here our satisfaction is not so perfect." Her criticism of his poetry was no less sharp: "His poems are mostly philosophical, which is not the truest kind of poetry. They want the simple force of nature and passion, and while they charm the ear and interest the mind, fail to wake far-off echoes in the heart."

Already she had broken with Emerson spiritually, though they continued intermittent communication. Her reviews in effect were a public farewell. Eventually he was to have revenge.

Until Margaret Fuller immigrated to New York at the age of thirty-four, her major emotional involvement had been with Emerson, whose craggy face and lanky form she greatly admired. She called him "my Druid." Her first adolescent crush had been her kinsman George T. Davis. When Davis married someone else, Margaret took to bed with a fever. Then Margaret, at eighteen, became infatuated with the fifteen-year-old beauty Anna Barker, kin of the Astors, sent from New York to Cambridge to acquire culture—a girl who in later years so titillated Emerson that he gushed about "that very human piece of divinity." A decade later, thinking of Anna, Margaret wrote musingly in her journal, "It is so true that a woman may be in love with a woman and a man with a man." After Anna came Samuel Gray Ward, called by Margaret her "Raffaello" because he was "so sensuous, so loving, and so lovely." The dénouement was too painful: Sam Ward married Anna Barker, not Margaret. Thus finally Margaret turned toward Emerson, a married man—with Margaret, in her way, rivalling Henry David Thoreau for the Sage of Concord's affections.

Margaret's "soul" relationship to Emerson came to a climax in the autumn of 1840, the time of the Ward-Barker wedding. Letters recently published for the first time have given a new dimension to this exchange, and it now appears that

Margaret and Waldo were far more intimate than anyone had guessed. Emerson carefully filed his correspondence, but all of Margaret's letters from this period disappeared—except one, and that one was a copy in Emerson's own handwriting, suggesting that he may have preferred to delete some sections. These fragments reveal that Margaret's emotions, though fever hot, were not caloric enough to melt the Emersonian glacier.

Toward the end of September, 1840, Emerson wrote that "certain crises must impend," and "perhaps it [is] better to part now. Now in your last letter you . . . do say . . . that I am yours & yours shall be, let me dally how long soever in this or that other temporary relation." Next day he entered in his journal, avoiding use of Margaret's name: "You would have me love you? What shall I love? Your body? The supposition disgusts you."

On the day of Emerson's letter Margaret was writing to her closest woman friend, Caroline Sturgis (with whom Emerson also corresponded): "Of the mighty changes in my spiritual life I do not wish to speak, yet surely you cannot be ignorant of them."

A few days later she wrote Waldo the letter he copied for his file: ". . . If you ever know me well, you will feel that the fact of my abiding by you thus far, affords a strong proof that we are to be much to one another. How often have I left you despairing & forlorn. How often have I said, This light will never understand my fire. . . . Could I lead the highest angel captive by a look, that look I would not give, unless prompted by true love: I am no usurper. . . . To L. [Lidian, Mrs. Emerson] my love. In her I have always recognized the saintly element. . . . Yet I am no saint, no anything, but a great soul born to know all."

A month later Margaret told Caroline in confidence: "I have just written a letter to our dear Waldo which gives me pain. . . . His call bids me return, I know not how, yet full of tender renunciation, know not how to refuse." Emerson's reply was unsparing: "I have your frank & noble & affecting letter, and yet I think I could wish it unwritten."

From this point on, all was a downward spiral. Margaret's assumption of the *Dial* editorship that same year increasingly consumed her energies. When, a year later, she was a houseguest at Emerson's home in Concord, she and the Sage preferred to confront each other by letter from room to room, rather than face to face. Emerson's small son, Waldo, was their courier. Balked by the impenetrable walls between them, Margaret wrote plaintively: "When I come to yourself, I cannot receive you, and you cannot give yourself; it does not profit." And: "There is nothing I wish more than to be able to live with you, without disturbing you."

Perhaps Margaret's acceptance of Greeley's *Tribune* offer in late 1844, in addition to her need to earn a living, was a gesture of defiance toward Emerson. In New York she was sufficiently free of "the Dear Wise One" to be able to search elsewhere for a soul mate. The likeliest prospect stemmed from the most unlikely quarter: a blue-eyed, blond German immigrant from Holstein, a businessman. James Nathan, whom she met at a literary soiree, was about her age, but from a family as orthodox in Judaism as hers was in Puritanism. He had two particular assets: a guitar, which he played with a romantic air, and an appealing dog named Josie.

Margaret had been invited by Mrs. Greeley to live at the Greeley farm on the outskirts of town. Aside from the fact that this location was difficult for a city suitor, Mr. Greeley did not much "take to" Nathan, and subterfuge became necessary. Margaret and Nathan were forced to meet in bookshops, tearooms, restaurants, and other public places, which retarded the development of intimacy.

Again Margaret resorted to the pen, composing a series of notes which are theatrical in comparison with her letters to Emerson, and fanciful in comparison with the love letters she was to write later in Italian. Evidently her inner eye seemed to be watching a play with a histrionic, grandly dramatic heroine. "I hear you with awe assert power over me and feel it to be true," she wrote. "It causes awe, but not dread, such as I felt sometimes since at the approach of this mysterious power, for I feel deep confidence in my friend and know that he will lead me on in a spirit of holy love. . . ."

However, he did not. The "affair" lasted only a few months, until Nathan hurriedly departed for Germany, leaving his dog with Margaret. Only gradually did she realize she had been abandoned; the disillusionment was bitter. She demanded the return of her letters, or that they be burned. Nathan refused. The letters weighed heavily on Margaret, but their existence did not become public knowledge until 1903. Sold by Nathan's son, they were published with an introduction by Julia Ward Howe and titled *The Love Letters of Margaret Fuller*. The more revealing Italian love letters remained almost totally unknown.

Psychically and physically exhausted, Margaret eagerly accepted the opportunity to go abroad as foreign correspondent for the *Tribune*. It was the old dream realized. Marcus and Rebecca Spring, wealthy Quaker friends, offered to pay Margaret's fare if she would accompany them and tutor their twelve-year-old son, and Greeley offered to pay eight to twelve dollars per dispatch.

On the first of August, 1846, they sailed aboard the *Cambria*, a sail-steam ship. It was a record crossing:

ten days sixteen hours Boston to Liverpool—symbolic of the new industrial revolution. But for Margaret, another, more important revolution was impending. In London, Paris, Rome, awaited the three men who would totally change her life.

In Britain *Woman in the Nineteenth Century* had been read with much sympathy, opening many doors for Margaret. She and the Springs undertook a leisurely tour by diligence, canal boat, and the new iron horse. She interviewed Harriet Martineau, Wordsworth, and De Quincey; inspected pubs, country estates, coal mines, castles, steel mills, public laundries, and, incidentally, got lost for an entire night on the Scottish mountain Ben Lomond. She was appalled by the poverty and the class distinctions, enchanted by the English countryside, furious at the working conditions in the mines and factories, shocked by the filth and hopelessness of the poor. Immediately she advocated a "peaceful revolution." She was emotionally and po-

Marchese Giovanni Angelo Ossoli

litically ready for the first real revolutionary she had ever met.

His name was Giuseppe Mazzini, an Italian exile living in England with a sentence of death on his head, an intellectual with intense, beautiful, fascinating eyes. He was five years Margaret's senior. He had organized poor immigrant boys into schools and clubs as part of his "Young Italy" movement. One evening Margaret addressed one of the groups, and Mazzini wrote to his mother that she "made a touching speech." He wrote other things, too, so glowing that his mother suggested that he should have Margaret live with him and care for him. But he was not to be diverted from revolution by even a Margaret Fuller.

Margaret for her part was swept entirely into his orbit. She found him "pure music." She wrote an article for the *Tribune* about Mazzini and his goals, reminding Americans that Italy was "the mother of our language and our laws, our greatest benefactress." Unaware of potential dangers, she joined a plot to smuggle Mazzini back into Italy as a member of the Springs' party—with an American passport. So secret was the scheme that past biographers generally have been unaware of it. The plan called for Mazzini to make contact with the Americans later in Paris, in disguise. To Margaret his parting admonition was far from political: "Learn to love not only Italy, but the Italians." She accepted this advice to a degree that perhaps astonished him.

In Paris, Margaret plunged, with her usual adventurousness, once more into a round of sightseeing, theatre, opera, interviews. She was invited to a court ball (King Louis Philippe). For a tooth extraction, she tried the new wonder drug, ether. Of the luminaries she met, George Sand (Madame Dudevant) and her lover, Chopin, were outstanding. In *Woman* Margaret had spoken favorably of George Sand as an emanci-

pated woman, bringing the wrath of the morally self-righteous down on her own head. Now she exercised caution and reported only to her spinster friend Elizabeth Hoar that George Sand "needs no defense, but only to be understood, for she has bravely acted out her nature." It was as if Margaret Fuller sought to prepare a brief in her own defense.

Well she might, for an ironic question posed to her in a letter from Mazzini's friend Adam Mickiewicz was pounding in her ears: "For you the first step of your deliverance . . . is to know whether you are to be permitted to remain a virgin." Like Mazzini an exile, Mickiewicz lived in Paris, banished from his Polish homeland by the Russian czar for revolutionary activities. At age forty-eight he was still strikingly handsome and of superb physique, his country's national poet, and a popular hero as well.

It is difficult to understand why Mickiewicz's letters have been overlooked as playing a decisive part in Margaret's European adventure. Certainly she recognized this "real and important relation," as she said. As for Mickiewicz, his sweeping appreciation of Margaret was in bold contrast to that of her niggardly New England colleagues: she was "the only woman to whom it has been given to touch what is decisive in the present world and to have a presentiment of the world of the future." He continued by letter to urge her physical liberation.

Mazzini, constantly spied upon, was forced to change his plans and did not come to Paris—fortunately for the American conspirators. But Margaret was deeply disappointed. In early spring, 1847, she and the Springs left Paris, heading for Naples. On the way a serious mishap occurred: their English steamer was rammed and nearly sunk by a coastal ship. Quite cavalierly Margaret described it all for her *Tribune* readers,

CONTINUED ON PAGE 94

47

PAUL MORPHY,
Chess Prodigy

Could he have beaten Bobby Fischer?

"Blindfolded"—that is, seated with his back to the chessboards—Paul Morphy once played as many as eight opponents simultaneously in 1858 at the Café de la Régence, a favorite hangout for chess experts in Paris. (He won six of those games, drew the others.) Morphy was twenty-one at the time. His portrait, above, by S. N. Carvalho, was painted two years later, after he quit competition.
TOP: BROWN BROS.; ABOVE: CULVER

Oliver Wendell Holmes once celebrated Americans as a people "which insists in sending out yachts and horses and boys to outsail, out-run, out-fight, and checkmate all the rest of creation." The concluding champion on his list was Paul Charles Morphy, whose youthful exploits in chess during the 1850's won the admiration of poets, scientists, and thousands of ordinary buffs.

Born in New Orleans on June 22, 1837, Morphy early showed a flair for chess. By the age of ten he had learned the moves of the game by watching—propped up on books so he could see the board—his aristocratic Creole relatives play at gatherings in the elegant Morphy home on Royal Street. He was the leading player in New Orleans by the age of twelve, when he won two games and drew one playing with the touring Hungarian master Johann Löwenthal.

"The child has never opened a work on chess. . . ." his uncle Ernest wrote. "In the openings he makes the right moves as if by inspiration; and it is astonishing to note the precision of his calculations in the middle and end game. When seated before the chessboard, his face betrays no agitation even in the most critical positions; in such cases he generally whistles through his teeth and patiently seeks for the combination to get him out of trouble. Further, he plays three or four severe games . . . without showing the least fatigue."

Morphy's father, who was a judge on the supreme court of Louisiana, allowed his son to play only on Sundays or, later, during school vacations. The boy showed as much promise at his studies as he did at chess. His academic career included a bachelor's degree with honors and an M.A. with highest honors from the Jesuit St. Joseph's College (now Spring Hill College) in Alabama, and completion of legal studies at the Law School of the University of Louisiana, where he memorized nearly all of the state's civil code. He achieved all this before his twentieth birthday.

48

By CHARLES L. CUTLER

Despite his father's strictures, Morphy became so skilled at chess that he was one of sixteen major players in the nation invited to enter the First American Chess Congress in New York, which started in October, 1857. His father had died a year earlier, and Morphy felt free to squander on chess the year he had to wait before reaching twenty-one, when he could practice law. He showed up in New York, five feet four inches tall, slim, and dark-haired. "In appearance," a niece wrote, "he was cold and distant, due to a certain degree to nearsightedness, but his coldness was only apparent, for he was exceedingly courteous and pleasant to all with whom he came in contact."

Players in the tournament, unhampered by a time limit, sometimes lingered over a single move for more than an hour. Morphy outsat—and outplayed—the best of them, losing only one game as he captured the title. He accepted his victory with nonchalance, then issued a challenge to anyone in the country for a match at odds of a pawn and the first move. By then he was president of the New Orleans Chess Club and occasionally played at odds of a knight or a rook. He sometimes also played "blindfolded," which most often meant seated with his back to the board; once he defeated seven opponents simultaneously in this fashion.

Morphy's fans in New Orleans asked Howard Staunton, the champion of Great Britain and a literary scholar, to visit New Orleans for a ten-thousand-dollar match with their hero. When Staunton begged off because of his work on a new edition of Shakespeare, Morphy's friends urged the young man to go to Europe and take on the greatest masters there.

Once in England, where he landed a day before his twenty-first birthday, Morphy lost no time proving to skeptics that his daring style—often climaxed by stunning sacrifices—worked as well against Europeans as Americans. The only top English player to remain unscathed was Staunton, who, with silence, ambiguity, and scornful comments, repeatedly fended off Morphy's challenges to play. Actually, Staunton's playing ability had declined, and he did not dare to confront the newcomer in a match.

Bitterly frustrated by Staunton's evasions, Morphy left for Paris after two and a half months in England. There he defeated experts at the Café de la Régence, the haunt of many great chess players, and soon he was the toast of Paris. In a dazzling display of blindfold playing, he took on eight opponents at once, defeating six and drawing with two. At the end, his secretary wrote, "Morphy stepped from the armchair in which he had been almost immovable for ten consecutive hours, without having tasted a morsel of anything, even water, during the whole period; yet as fresh, apparently, as when he sat down."

Morphy's crowning achievement came when Adolf Anderssen, the unofficial world champion (there was no official title until later in the century), arrived from Germany to play him. Leaving a sickbed for the match, Morphy won by seven wins to two losses, with two draws. When someone tried to console Anderssen afterward by telling him that he had not played up to form, he replied: "No, Morphy won't let me. It is no use struggling against him; he is like a piece of machinery which is sure to come to a certain conclusion."

Morphy's return to New York on May 11, 1859, was the signal for patriotic rejoicing by American intellectuals. Well-wishers held a testimonial gathering at the chapel of New York University and presented him with a set of solid gold and silver chessmen made by Tiffany. The Union Chess Club crowned the self-possessed young man with a silver wreath. And later, at a banquet in Boston attended by Brahmins and Harvard scholars, James Russell Lowell offered a toast in verse to Morphy:

I give you the man who can think out and dare
His bloodless Marengos on twelve inches
square,
Yet so modest, the conquered all feel that
they meet
With a Morphy—and not morti-fying
defeat.

Back in New Orleans, Morphy quit chess competition to establish himself as a lawyer. But he gave up this undertaking because the public could not believe a world chess champion would find their legal difficulties worthy of attention. Nothing else seemed to go right. A beautiful heiress whom Morphy, through a friend, approached about marriage declared she could not consider marrying "a mere chess player." With the outbreak of the Civil War Morphy tried to get appointed to a diplomatic post with the Confederacy. He was rejected again.

Morphy's family fled New Orleans when Union soldiers arrived. They spent the war years in Havana and in Paris, which Morphy loved. But frustration over the Staunton episode, the heights he had scaled and abandoned as a chess genius, the impact of the Civil War—all left Morphy dejected.

His worried mother sent him to Paris again in 1867, hoping that a change of scenery would restore his spirits. He came back little better. In 1869 Morphy ended even the private games of chess he had enjoyed with a close friend. His melancholy gave way to a paranoia that led him to suspect relatives and friends of trying to steal his clothes, rob him of his inheritance, and poison his food. Over the next fifteen years he became firmly fixed as a local character—a dapper little man with haunted eyes, strolling through the city by day and appearing at the opera by night.

On July 10, 1884, at the age of forty-seven, Paul Morphy—genius and riddle—died of apoplexy.

Charles L. Cutler, who is an editor for American Education Publications, won runner-up honors as a youth in the Massachusetts junior chess championship.

Walter Lord:
HUMILIATION

THE YEAR WAS 1814,
AND WITHIN THREE WEEKS
OUR "YOUNG AND NOT
ALWAYS WISE" NATION
SUFFERED ACUTE SHAME
AND WAS REVIVED BY
AN ASTONISHING VICTORY

THE FALL of WASHINGTON — or Mad...

AMERICAN HERITAGE BOOK SELECTION

and TRIUMPH

This wordy cartoon, published in London in October, 1814, shows two British hearties and some glum Americans, all mocking Madison for having fled his burning capital. The President is not shown, but the two men at center, strewing documents as they flee the flames, are Cabinet members annoyed at being deprived of their expected victory supper.

ANNE S. K. BROWN MILITARY COLLECTION, BROWN UNIVERSITY

Caught in the crossfire of the Napoleonic conflict, America declared war on Great Britain in 1812 for what seemed to the government to be ample reason. The young Republic's trade had been stifled, her seamen impressed, her ships seized by the Royal Navy. Western settlers feared British intrigue among the Indians. Canada, in contrast, loomed as an ever more inviting target for land-hungry "war hawks."

For two years the war sputtered along, mostly on the Canadian front, usually a bloody stalemate. Then, in the spring of 1814, came a dramatic development. Napoleon collapsed, freeing thousands of "Wellington's Invincibles" for service elsewhere and allowing London for the first time to turn its full attention on the brash upstart across the Atlantic.

Good Britons relished the prospect. They felt they had been fighting for freedom—everybody's freedom—only to be knifed in the back by their own ungrateful progeny. Now it was time to "chastise Jonathan."

Heavy reinforcements were soon on their way to Canada. At the same time, a separate expedition headed across the Atlantic to strike directly at America's eastern seaboard. This consisted of some four thousand crack Peninsular veterans led by Major General Robert Ross and under the overall command of Vice Admiral Sir Alexander Cochrane, Commander in Chief of the North American Station. Cochrane planned to use the force, together with his Royal Marines and ships, first in operations along the Atlantic coast, later in an attack on New Orleans. Strategic considerations came first, of course, but prize money was never very far from the Admiral's mind.

On August 16 the expedition swept through the Virginia Capes, up the Chesapeake Bay, and joined the squadron of Rear Admiral George Cockburn, a jaunty sea dog who knew the area well. Cockburn urged that they land at Benedict, a small Maryland town on the Patuxent River, attack Commodore Joshua Barney's gunboat flotilla, which had been trapped forty miles upstream, and then, if all went well, strike a blow at Washington itself. At the same time Captain James Gordon would lead a small squadron up the Potomac to divert the Americans and cover the main force if anything went wrong.

Cochrane agreed, and on August 19 the troops began landing at Benedict. On the twentieth they headed up the river, accompanied by the boats of the fleet. On the twenty-second they forced Barney to scuttle his flotilla.

On the twenty-third they swung west for Bladensburg, just northeast of the District of Columbia line.

Meanwhile, the little new city of Washington desperately tried to organize some sort of resistance. There had been warnings all summer; a special military district had been set up under Brigadier General William H. Winder; and thousands of troops had been earmarked for the defense of the capital—but all this was misleading. Actually the troops were mostly raw militia, the requisitions largely just paper, the Secretary of War, John Armstrong, unbelievably complacent, and General Winder a hopeless incompetent. The sixty-three-year-old President, James Madison, had a brilliant mind but was far from a gifted war leader, and sometimes it seemed that the only person with real spirit was his indomitable wife Dolley.

No real resistance had yet developed when Washington learned on the morning of August 24 that the British were approaching Bladensburg, virtually at the gates of the city. The President, the Cabinet, General Winder, the District militia, Barney's stranded flotilla men—some three thousand men altogether—raced to the little town. Here they joined another three thousand Maryland militia already on the scene. The combined force was still being deployed when the British appeared.

It was all over in a couple of hours. Sweeping forward, General Ross's little army scattered one militia detachment after another. Only Barney's men put up a good resistance, but in the end they, too, were overwhelmed, with the Commodore wounded and a prisoner. Washington lay open for the taking. . . .

—W.L.

PART **1**

HUMILIATION
AT
WASHINGTON

From a third-floor window in his handsome house on Capitol Hill, Dr. James Ewell studied the horizon, searching for some clue to the course of battle at Bladensburg. Occasionally he could see a puff of smoke, or hear the distant rumble of guns, but that was all. It was impossible to guess what was going on.

Gradually the smoke and rumble died away, and for a while there was just silence. Then for the first time the doctor noticed a cloud of dust over the outskirts of the city—a cloud that grew steadily thicker and nearer. Soon soldiers began running by—at first in twos and threes, then in swarms. At one point Ewell caught a glimpse of Secretary of War John Armstrong himself, almost lost in the mob. A horseman rode by, shouting warnings of rape. The doctor's daughters began screaming, and Mrs. Ewell sobbed over and over, "What shall we do? What shall we do?"

On the other side of the city Superintendent of Patents William Thornton and his wife also scanned the horizon from their house on F Street. They knew the troops were engaged, but they lived farther away than the Ewells and could hear nothing. At last they saw a man riding hard up Pennsylvania Avenue toward the President's House—clearly a messenger bringing news of some sort.

At the President's House a servant boy named Paul Jennings was busy getting dinner ready. Madison had indicated that most of the Cabinet and a few "military gentlemen" would be coming, so Jennings carefully set the table, brought up the ale, wine, and cider, and placed the bottles in coolers. He was just about finished when, around three o'clock, Madison's freedman servant Jim Smith galloped up to the house, waving his hat and shouting, "Clear out, clear out! General Armstrong has ordered a retreat!"

Mrs. Madison had been waiting all day for some word from her husband. Twice, Washington's Mayor James Blake turned up, urging her to leave, but she hung on, hoping for the best, spending much of her time at an upper window turning a spyglass in every direction. She saw little then, but Jim Smith's spectacular arrival made everything all too clear. As if his excited cries weren't enough, he brought a hastily pencilled note from Madison. It said the battle was lost . . . fly at once.

But above all, Dolley Madison was a woman of composure, and she wasn't about to leave without attending to a few important details first. By now her sister and brother-in-law, Mr. and Mrs. Richard Cutts, were on hand—also the New York banker Jacob Barker, Presidential aide Charles Carroll of Bellevue, and one or two other gallants—and she turned to them for help. Together they all went to work, trying to save what they could on the spur of the moment.

Somebody found a wagon, and they quickly loaded it with most of the silver, some papers, a few books, a small clock, the red velvet curtains from the drawing room. In minutes the load was on its way to the Bank of Maryland, safely beyond the city.

What took time was the full-length portrait of Washington, which was hanging on the west wall of the dining room. Attributed to Gilbert Stuart, it was the showpiece of the mansion. All agreed that it would be a crowning disgrace if it fell into British hands. Only the previous day the President had assured George Washington Custis that the painting would be taken care of in any emergency. Now the President's wife considered it her special responsibility.

But nobody could get it down. The Madisons' versatile French doorkeeper Jean Pierre Sioussa and the gardener Tom Magraw tugged and twisted, but it was screwed too tightly to the wall. Charles Carroll and Jacob Barker tried their hand but had no better luck.

Minutes ticked by, and Carroll grew impatient. Forget the picture, he scolded Mrs. Madison, she must leave right away. Otherwise she was bound to be trapped among the retreating troops already pouring by the house.

She wasn't ready to give up yet. Magraw worked on, teetering at the top of a ladder, while Sioussa rushed off to get an axe. Finally they chopped the frame apart, took out the canvas, still on its stretcher, and laid it on the dining-room floor. By now Carroll was gone—off to rejoin the President—so Mrs. Madison turned to Barker and Robert G. L. de Peyster, another New Yorker standing by.

"Save that picture," she said. "Save that picture if possible. If not possible, destroy it. Under no circumstances allow it to fall into the hands of the British." At the same time she begged them to rescue the ornamental eagles in the drawing room and four remaining boxes of the President's papers.

Now, at last, she felt free to go. Stuffing a few more pieces of silverware into her netted reticule, she hurried out the door and

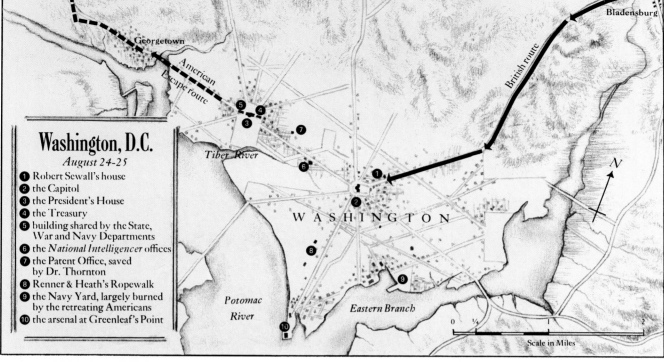

BY ROBERT RITTER FOR *The Dawn's Early Light* (NORTON, 1972)

Washington, D.C.
August 24-25

1. Robert Sewall's house
2. the Capitol
3. the President's House
4. the Treasury
5. building shared by the State, War and Navy Departments
6. the *National Intelligencer* offices
7. the Patent Office, saved by Dr. Thornton
8. Renner & Heath's Ropewalk
9. the Navy Yard, largely burned by the retreating Americans
10. the arsenal at Greenleaf's Point

into a waiting carriage. Her personal maid Sukey jumped in beside her, and with coachman Joe Bolin at the reins, they rolled onto Pennsylvania Avenue and headed out of the city. About the same time, another carriage left with the Cuttses, and the President's coachee brought up the rear. Madison always considered this a most unsatisfactory vehicle, but his butler John Freeman was only too glad to have it now. Piling in his family, he drove off with a feather bed lashed to the rear.

While Dolley Madison galloped westward for safety, the President was caught in the maelstrom of defeat swirling back from Bladensburg. High and low—the statesmen, the generals, the soldiers and sailors, the "private gentlemen"—they all reeled back together. General William Henry Winder, military commander of the district, worked frantically to collect enough of his demoralized army to defend Washington. Finding no organized force waiting, or even in evidence, at the edge of the city, he gave the order to retreat again.

It was the third call for retreat in an hour, and the men were more discouraged than ever as they streamed down Maryland Avenue and spread out on the rough stubble of the Capitol grounds.

Secretary of State James Monroe and Secretary Armstrong, arriving separately, joined Winder; and while everyone watched and waited the three huddled over what to do next. Armstrong favored the idea of turning the Capitol into a citadel and holding out indefinitely. He liked those strong limestone walls; he didn't mind the big windows or the fact that the place was really two separate buildings. At this stage in its construction, only the House and Senate wings were finished, connected by a vulnerable wooden passageway. To him it was safe enough, and he pointed out that the British didn't have the artillery to conduct a serious siege.

Winder would have none of it. He had too small a force. The men were too exhausted. The Capitol was too isolated. He could be starved out in twenty-four hours. Even if he managed to hold the place, the British would be free to roam at will through the rest of Washington. His only hope was to retreat again, this time to the heights behind Georgetown. Here at last he'd be safe. Probably some of the Maryland militia routed at Bladensburg would come there, too, and he would have a real chance to collect and reorganize the shattered army.

Monroe backed him up. In fact, he added a point. During the retreat from Bladensburg the Secretary of State thought he had detected a powerful British column moving to the west. He feared that if the Americans delayed at the Capitol any longer, they might be driven into a cul-de-sac between the Eastern Branch and the Potomac.

Outvoted and half-convinced, Armstrong concurred.

So it was retreat again. And now the last semblance of discipline vanished. Many of the men had stood by this long only because they were from the District. Their sole purpose had been to save their homes and families. Falling back to Georgetown was no way to do that. A few raged—even wept—but most simply scattered to look after their own interests.

The rest streamed up Pennsylvania Avenue in no order whatsoever. Francis Scott Key, a Washington lawyer serving as a military aide, rode by—his horse steaming, his uniform soaked with sweat. Secretary Armstrong tried to dodge an angry citizen named Thomas Ewell, who rushed up shouting that Armstrong was to blame for everything. At Hughes's grocery near Seventh Street the crowd swarmed around the pump. Some were content with the water; others preferred a barrel of whiskey thoughtfully provided by John P. Van Ness, formerly the commander of the District's militia.

Suddenly a voice cried, "There goes the President!" It was true. Back from the shambles of Bladensburg, James Madison had transferred to a carriage and was now rolling through the crowd on Pennsylvania Avenue. Ultimately, he arrived at the President's House around 4:30—about half an hour after his wife had left—accompanied by several aides who had been with him most of the day. Entering, they found Jacob Barker and Robert de Peyster collecting a few final valuables, and for more than an hour the group sat around exchanging experiences. It was an odd interlude, with the British just over the horizon and the city clearly doomed, and can best be explained by the sixty-three-year-old President's desperate need for rest after his grim, long day in the saddle.

The conversation was appropriately serious. Madison was especially awed by the superb discipline of the British army. Like most Jeffersonians, he had relished the theory that the free democratic yeoman fighting for his home was always a match for the mere paid hireling of a foreign foe. Now he knew better. "I could never have believed," he told Barker, "that so great a difference existed between regular troops and a militia force, if I had not witnessed the scenes of this day."

In contrast with this quiet post-mortem, the scene outside was increasingly raucous. The collapse of all discipline, the knowledge that the city was lost, and perhaps a little of John P. Van Ness's whiskey did their work. The fleeing soldiers and civilians began rummaging through the government offices, taking what they wanted. At the President's House the guards stationed at the door had long since run off, and stragglers roamed at will through the mansion. Someone even stole a pair of pistols that the weary President had taken from their holsters and left on a front-hall table.

Clearly it was time to go. The plan had been for the Madisons to join forces with Secretary of the Navy William Jones and his family at Bellevue, the Carroll house, but now that was out. It would be simpler and safer to meet at Foxhall's foundry by the river, and an aide was sent ahead to alert everyone. But no sooner had he gone than this plan was changed, too; probably it was felt that the sooner the President got across the river, the safer he would be. Finally, Madison and his party rode across the meadow behind the President's House and down to the river. Here, at Mason's Ferry, they took a boat over to Analostan Island and then went by the causeway to the Virginia shore.

Barker and de Peyster remained at the mansion, continuing their last-minute effort to save a few more things. At one point a group of exhausted soldiers stopped by, and they took time out to break open some of the President's brandy. The big por-

trait of George Washington still lay attached to its stretcher on the dining-room floor.

The time had now come to do something about it. Dolley Madison had said not to roll it up, and they would follow her instructions. Recruiting two blacks, the four of them carefully lifted the whole framework, carried it through the front door, and loaded it on a cart that had miraculously been found. Tossing in some large silver urns and a few other odds and ends, they set off up Pennsylvania Avenue in the midst of the fleeing crowd.

In the President's House Sioussa went about the last duties of a good doorkeeper. He carefully hid some gold and silver Algerian pistols that looked as though they might make good loot. Next, he put out buckets of water and some bottles of wine for any more thirsty soldiers who might happen by. Then he picked up the mansion's pet macaw—a great favorite of Dolley Madison's—and took it a few blocks to Colonel John Tayloe's Octagon House.

Now back to the President's House for a final look around. Everything seemed in order, so he carefully closed all the windows and doors. Then he departed for the last time, leaving the front-door key at the house of the Russian Minister, Daschkoff, who had wisely gone to Philadelphia.

Some two hundred fifty to three hundred of Joshua Barney's men were still at the Capitol, without orders. Winder never considered them part of his own command, as they were really naval personnel; and with the Commodore wounded and a prisoner, there was really nobody to tell them what to do. While the men lay exhausted in the square Captain Bacon of the Marines and Captain Gohegan of the flotilla wrangled over who had command.

Captain Thomas Tingey at the Navy Yard was another officer whom Winder left in the dark. Here it was not a question of command—Tingey clearly came under naval authority; but close coordination was all-important so that he would know if and when to carry out his careful plans for demolishing the installation. The General never sent a word.

Secretary Armstrong learned of the lapse just before setting out himself for Frederick, Maryland, where the government was supposed to reconvene once the British had taken the city. There wasn't time to do much, but he did send Major John Bell to Tingey with a verbal message that was crystal clear in its brevity: "The Navy Yard cannot be covered."

This announcement was punctuated a few moments later by a loud explosion. Captain John O. Creighton had blown up the main bridge over the Eastern Branch. Then a great cloud of smoke rose as the wreckage began burning.

Tingey quickly warned the families still living in the neighborhood that the Navy Yard would go next, the fires might spread, better save what they could.

Quiet slowly settled over the city. Here and there a few people still scurried about on last-minute missions. The mood was sombre at Francis Scott Key's house on Bridge Street in Georgetown. Key had arrived home exhausted and was now begging his wife and children to leave. He himself felt duty bound to stay, but it was no place for them. Polly Key would have none of it. The most Key could do was pack their things. Then he bolted all the windows and the family sat in the stifling heat, half expecting the British to come any minute.

Where were they anyhow? At the time the battle ended, there wasn't a fleeing American who didn't feel that some red-coat was personally following him. Yet four hours had passed, and not an enemy soldier in sight. In the silence of the August twilight the jitters steadily grew. Mrs. William Thornton, riding north out of Georgetown, was warned to turn back—the British were purposely herding the American Army that way and planned to fall on them. A delegation of leading Georgetown citizens headed out to obtain the best terms possible but could find no one to surrender to.

Another rumor had the British approaching by the race track, out Fourteenth Street, but there was no one there either. According to a third story, they were down by the Marine barracks on the other side of town—"the whistling of the balls had been distinctly heard"—but again, there was nothing to it. Late in the afternoon still another account put them at the Capitol, in full force. A young officer arrived at the Navy Yard saying it was true. If so, this was getting dangerously close, and Captain Tingey made ready to light his fuses.

His chief clerk, Mordecai Booth, exploded in indignation, using language quite out of character for this faithful but docile underling. He had just been to the Capitol on a reconnaissance of his own, and he *knew* the British weren't there. It would be a crime to destroy the Yard on such false information. In fact he felt it would be a crime to destroy it anyhow; it could so easily be defended by recruiting some of Barney's now leaderless men and using the numerous guns on hand.

Booth offered to ride out and find where the British really were if only Tingey would hold off his demolitions a little longer. Very well, said the captain, adding that the intelligence had better be good, his whole career was resting on it.

Booth quickly rode to the turnpike gate and studied the rolling country in the direction of Bladensburg. Nothing in sight. Then a lone horseman suddenly came in view, racing down the turnpike toward him. It was a Georgetown butcher named Thomas Miller. He had been looking for the British, too, had found exactly where they were, and would be happy to show them to Booth. The two rode to the top of a nearby hill, and Miller pointed out a long column of troops slowly advancing toward them. They wore the dark blue of British seamen, but Booth knew nothing about that. Like most Americans, he assumed every hostile Englishman was invariably dressed in red, and he now argued that these must be a Georgetown rifle company still in the field. A shot whizzed by his ears, ending the discussion.

Galloping back to the Navy Yard, he informed Captain Tingey. Momentarily, at least, the news took a little pressure off the captain: the British were not as close as he had feared. Perhaps he could still save the Yard if only he knew where the American troops were. Except for Armstrong's terse warning, nobody had told him anything.

Once again Booth rode out, this time to the President's House. He supposed that Madison was still there, and if anybody knew where the Army was, it ought to be the nation's Commander in Chief. Arriving at the mansion, he found only an agitated cavalry colonel standing by the steps. In the gathering dark the officer assumed Booth was the advance guard of the enemy and pulled his pistol. It was all Booth could do to persuade him they were both on the same side.

To Booth, that dark empty house, standing alone in the dusk, said far more than a bundle of intelligence reports. For the first time he fully realized that the capital of his country had been completely abandoned.

By the time he reached Capitol Hill again, several stray horsemen had joined up. These included a trooper named Walter Cox and Navy Captain John O. Creighton, who had also been sent out by Tingey to gather information. It was now quite dark, and as the party approached Long's Hotel on A Street, N.E., Cox leaned far forward in his saddle. He was clearly trying to make something out. Only cows, Booth remarked. Yes, Cox replied, he saw the cows, but he also saw *men* . . . right there, rising out of that hollow.

They were there all right. Within forty yards. The little group wheeled and scattered wildly for safety. Booth and Creighton dashed for the Navy Yard to warn Captain Tingey.

Lieutenant James Scott decided that all resistance was over as he rode through the gathering darkness with the British advance guard, led by Major General Robert Ross himself. Leaving Bladensburg at twilight after a three-hour rest, they found the Americans had disappeared completely.

And now Washington lay at their feet, the climax of the week's campaign. It was a soldier's dream of triumph—the capture of the enemy capital—yet there was no trace of martial glory: no bands, no banners, no grand entrance, no conquered boulevards lined with a sullen, beaten populace. The city lay dark and empty, its sprinkling of houses and buildings looking (in the words of a contemporary visitor) "as if some giant had scattered a box of child's toys upon the ground."

Only the 3rd Brigade was making the march. Consisting of the seamen, marines, and most of the 21st Foot—some 1,460 men altogether—they had seen little action and were fresh and rested. The other brigades would follow along later, after reorganization. Entering the city, most of the troops halted just inside the turnpike gate, while Ross, Rear Admiral George Cockburn, and a small advance guard continued forward. Moving down Maryland Avenue, they headed directly for the Capitol.

At some point the two commanders had decided to lay the city under contribution as the price of sparing it, and now a drum rolled loud and long, sounding the call for a parley. If any American heard, he either didn't understand this military refinement or chose to ignore it, for there was no answer whatsoever.

The little British party rode on, halting at a point perhaps two hundred yards short of the Capitol. Directly to their right stood the large brick house owned by Robert Sewall. Other buildings loomed in the darkness. Not a light or a sound came from any of them.

The Admiral and the General conferred, wondering what to do next. A few more seconds, then a volley of musket fire shattered the night. Four men were hit—one killed—and Ross's horse was shot from under him. It was hard to see where the firing came from—but certainly from Robert Sewall's house and possibly other buildings, too.

Splinters flew as Lieutenant Scott led the party that broke through Sewall's front door. But it took several minutes, and by the time the men got in, the house was completely empty. No one ever knew who fired the shots. Later, most accounts attributed it to a few diehards led by a local barber named Dixon, but it seems more likely that some of Barney's flotilla men were responsible. They never considered themselves bound by Winder's orders to retreat, and many of them were on the Capitol grounds long after the army had gone.

Whoever they were, British reaction was swift. Cockburn raced back to the turnpike gate to get the light companies of the 21st Foot, and Michael Shiner—a local black, hence according to British policy left alone—watched with fascination as the troops fired their Congreve rockets into the house. Beams and rafters went flying in all directions.

But no one looked at the blaze for long. Already the glare of a far bigger fire was creeping across the sky to the south. Soon billows of flame and smoke were gushing upward. Deep explosions shook the ground, and embers shot like comets through the blackness of the night.

Captain Tingey was burning his Navy Yard. For the colorful, headstrong commandant, it was a bitter moment indeed. Head of the yard since its founding in 1800, he had made it the finest in the country. By now he regarded it as practically his own—so much so that he had even included the Commandant's House in his will.

Yet orders were orders, and it had to go. Alerted by Mordecai Booth and Captain Creighton that the enemy were deep in the city, he finally gave the signal at 8:20 P.M. The matches were struck and the powder trains lit, leading to the storehouses and the sail loft. Kindled by the carpet of chips and pitch that covered the ground, the flames raced along, leaping from building to building—the sawmill, the rigging loft, the paint shops, the timber shed. Along with the rest went the new frigate *Columbia*, almost ready for launching, and the sloop of war *Argus*, completely finished.

Grimly satisfied that his duty was done, Captain Tingey stepped into his gig and rowed for Alexandria.

The brilliant glare from the Navy Yard made the job easier for General Ross's men on Capitol Hill. As one group burned Sewall's house others turned their attention to the rest of the nearby buildings. A stern-looking officer rode up to Andrew Hunter's door and began interrogating Mrs. Hunter. Where was her husband? Not at home. When did he leave? In the morning. Why? To take the children from this "horrid scene." When would he be back? She didn't know. Desperately, she invited him to go to the sideboard and help himself, then gingerly asked a question of her own: Did the British plan to burn the city generally, or only the public buildings? The officer said that all depended: where no resistance was made, private property would be safe, especially if everyone remained at home. But wherever there was resistance, or arms found, that place would be burned.

Outside, that policy was once again being demonstrated. Searching Tomlinson's Hotel, across from the Senate wing of the Capitol, Ross's men found guns and ammunition. It was instantly set on fire.

Now for the Capitol itself. The 3rd Brigade was quickly deployed in the square facing the building. A sharp command, and they fired a volley into the windows of the eastern façade. The practical purpose was, of course, to discourage any further sharpshooting, but it all seemed symbolic as well. It served as a formal announcement that this citadel of republicanism was being officially possessed in the name of His Majesty the King.

Stepping forward, Lieutenant de Lacy Evans led a party that quickly broke down the doors, and for the next hour the troops turned sightseers, roaming through the empty halls and chambers. Admiral Cockburn took a small bound copy of a Treasury report, which he kept as a souvenir. Someone with more extravagant tastes cut out the portraits of Louis XVI and Marie Antoinette hanging in the room adjoining the Senate chamber.

Lieutenant Scott took nothing, but he, too, was among the sightseers, staring with awe at Benjamin Latrobe's handsome Corinthian columns in the Hall of Representatives. It all seemed so much more grandiose than the cramped quarters of the House of Commons back home. He rather suspected that this nation which boasted so loudly of its republican simplicity was actually "somewhat infected with an unseemly bias for monarchial splendour."

The prospect of destroying this ambitious building raised no qualms—the British leaders in America were committed to the destruction or ransom of public property—but it did raise a question of method. The Capitol was so well built it seemed to defy burning. At first Ross and Cockburn were inclined to blow the place up, but word spread to the few remaining citizens in the neighborhood. They bitterly protested that the explosion would wreck their homes, too, and they had done nothing to oppose the British. The General relented; he would rely on the torch.

Naval Lieutenant George Pratt was put in charge. He was considered an expert at this sort of business, but at first things went rather slowly. In the House wing, three-man teams tackled each room on the lower floor. The first chopped the woodwork into kindling; the second sprinkled a bucket of rocket powder about; and the third applied the torch. This started a number of local fires, but nothing spectacular.

Upstairs, Pratt was having little better luck with the House chamber. At first his men fired rockets into the roof, but nothing happened. It turned out to be covered with sheet iron. Finally they piled the mahogany chairs, desks, and tables high in the center of the room, added some of the rocket powder, and fired more rockets directly into the pile. Similar measures were taken with the Senate wing, and Lieutenant Pratt's efforts were at last rewarded.

Within minutes both wings were ablaze. The limestone outer

walls might only crumble and crack, but there was more than enough to burn inside: the red morocco chairs of the Senate, the secret journals of the House—so carefully locked in a special drawer—the law library of Elias Bardinot Caldwell, clerk of the Supreme Court, the baize curtains of the House, the 740 books purchased in Europe in 1802 as a nucleus for the Library of Congress, the handsome gilt eagle surmounting the clock above the Speaker's chair, and the clock itself, whose hands pointed to 10 P.M. as the fire began.

Flames surged through the doors and windows, up through the roof, and fanned out into the night. The Navy Yard might make a better pyrotechnic display, but this was far more disastrous. The southwesterly breeze caught the sparks and carried them toward the streets to the north and east. Four more buildings were soon blazing, among them two houses built by George Washington on North Capitol Street.

To the British 1st and 2nd brigades, now approaching the city, the glare from the fires was so bright the men could easily recognize each other's faces. "Except for the burning of San Sebastian," Lieutenant George Robert Gleig later wrote, "I do not recollect to have witnessed, at any period of my life, a scene more striking or more sublime."

Dr. James Ewell, who had taken his family to the house of a Mrs. Orr, several blocks from his own house, heard a noise like thunder as the fire burst through the roof of the Capitol, then was even more startled by a tremendous pounding on the Orr front door. Five or six British soldiers tramped in, but to Mrs. Ewell's relief it was not rape they were after—only a little food. Their hosts instantly produced a cold ham, bread and butter, wine—anything that might keep them satisfied.

Then a new cause for alarm. Glancing outside, Ewell saw every room of his own house lit up with flames. He dashed to the scene, hoping to save his medical library, and happily discovered that it was just the glass in his windows reflecting the fire at the Capitol.

But the house had been plundered, and as Ewell contemplated the shambles the Reverend Alexander McCormack, rector of nearby Christ Church, came up and offered to take him to General Ross and Admiral Cockburn. Perhaps they could help, the minister suggested; he had met them and they were "perfect gentlemen."

Walking down the street a few steps, they approached an officer heavy with braid and lace. Putting on his best church manners, McCormack performed the honors, introducing Ewell to "General Ross."

"My name is Cockburn, sir," came the answer in the quick, high-pitched voice of the Admiral.

That straightened out, Ewell explained his troubles, saying he thought private property was safe; yet his was stolen, even though left in the care of servants.

"Well, sir," said the Admiral, "let me tell you it was very ill confidence to repose your property in the care of servants."

With this brief lecture on the dangers of the servant class, the Admiral seemed inclined to let the matter drop, but at this point Ross came up and was far more sympathetic. If Ewell would point out the house, he'd post a sentry there.

To the General's amiable embarrassment, it turned out to be the very house he had picked for his headquarters. Ross gallantly declared he "could never think of trespassing on the re-

pose of a private family." He would order his things out at once.

Ewell was no fool. Realizing that his best bet was to keep the General there, he begged him to stay. Ross finally consented—any small room would do—but the doctor gave him his own bedroom, the one with the good mattress.

The General wasn't ready for bed just yet. Parting with Dr. Ewell, he and Cockburn gathered together a small force of perhaps 150 picked men, and with each commanding a separate detachment, they started up Pennsylvania Avenue about 10:30 P.M. A single officer on foot led the way. Behind, the men marched two abreast, swiftly but silently. When somebody started talking, the officer broke in sharply: "Silence! If any man speaks in the ranks, I'll put him to death!"

Here and there along the avenue the bolder citizens peeked from open windows. As William P. Gardner watched them pass his place, four officers on horseback rode up and politely said good-evening.

Then one of them, Admiral Cockburn, asked pleasantly, "Where is your President, Mr. Madison?"

Gardner said he didn't know, but supposed he was by now far away. After a few minutes more of casual conversation, the officers excused themselves, explaining they were on their way to "pay a visit" to the President's House, which they understood was a little way ahead.

Soon they were at the Fifteenth Street "bend," where the avenue was interrupted by the grounds of the executive mansion. Here the force halted while arrangements were made at a boarding house kept by Mrs. Barbara Suter for a late supper for General Ross and his staff. Then on again, up Fifteenth Street, while the dismayed Mrs. Suter set about killing chickens and warming bread.

Now another stop, this time near the Treasury pump. While the troops crowded around, ignoring officers' warnings of poisoned water, Admiral Cockburn sent a thoughtful message ahead. Not knowing Dolley Madison's movements, he offered her an escort to any place of safety she might choose. But she was gone, of course, and there was no need for further amenities. The force moved on to the President's House.

Nothing startled them like the dining room. There the table was perfectly set for forty people. The servant boy Paul Jennings had done his work well—the wine stood in the coolers, packed in ice. Sampling cold cuts and what Captain Harry Smith termed "super-excellent Madeira," the unexpected guests hugely enjoyed themselves. The crystal goblets were raised in a joyous toast to "the health of the Prince Regent and success to His Majesty's arms by sea and land."

Cockburn had a special joke. Somewhere along the way he had corralled the Washington book dealer Roger Chew Weightman—probably impressed as a guide. Now the Admiral plopped the miserable Mr. Weightman down in a chair and told him to drink to "Jemmy," as Cockburn almost invariably called the President.

That over, the Admiral expansively told his victim to help himself to a souvenir. Weightman suggested something valuable, but Cockburn said no, the expensive things must feed the flames, and handed him instead a few odds and ends off a mantelpiece. The Admiral himself chose an old hat of the President's and a cushion off Mrs. Madison's chair—joking that the latter would remind him of her seat, or so a letter written three days later delicately implied.

By now, others, too, had joined the souvenir hunt. Ranging from Madison's medicine chest to a pair of rhinestone shoe buckles, the variety was endless. Captain Harry Smith was more practical: he went upstairs and, taking off his grimy, sweat-stained shirt, helped himself to the Presidential best. Downstairs, a soldier swept the plates and silver into a tablecloth and made off with the evening's best haul. Outside, the guards—unable to join the fun—amused themselves by hacking up an abandoned carriage.

The job of starting the fire was turned over to the efficient Lieutenant Pratt. His sailors quickly got torches from Nordin's beer house opposite the Treasury, and once again the familiar scene unfolded. The huge dining-room sideboard, the red velvet cushions of the Oval Room, the pianoforte from Andrew Hazlehurst, the President's half-filled portmanteau, the twenty-eight-dollar guitar—all of it went up in one roaring bonfire.

As the flames soared skyward the force turned its attention to the long brick Treasury building just to the east. The men had high hopes here, taking the name literally, and felt almost cheated when they found no money at all. But there were plenty of old records to burn—some going back to the Revolution—and the building was soon blazing nicely.

Now at last the night's work was done. General Ross and his staff retired to Mrs. Suter's for their prearranged dinner and were soon joined by Admiral Cockburn.

Following the meal, Admiral Cockburn was heading back down Pennsylvania Avenue when he had an afterthought. Hailing a man standing outside McKeowin's Hotel, the Admiral asked where he could find the offices of the *National Intelligencer*. The editor, Joseph Gales, Jr., whom he liked to call Dear Josey, had been very tough on him, and now there was a score to settle.

The man hailed was Chester Bailey, the contractor who ran the New York-Philadelphia mail stage. Pleading that he was a stranger in town, he said he had no idea where the paper's offices were. Actually, he knew perfectly well that they were right across the street.

Cockburn turned to two other bystanders, who also equivocated. Whatever else he might be, the Admiral was no fool, and he made it clearly understood that he wanted no more of this nonsense.

The bystanders got the point, and showed him the building themselves. A soldier then broke into the office and emerged with the last issue of the paper, assuring its readers that the city was safe. General Ross attempted to keep it as a souvenir but couldn't fit it into his pocket. "Damn it," he said, allowing himself a rare vulgarity, "my pocket is full of old Madison's love letters; I have no room for this trash."

Cockburn now ordered the building burned, but at this point he was confronted by two ladies who lived in the block. They begged him to hold off, or their houses would go, too. The Ad-

miral listened carefully, and finally agreed not to burn the place down. Instead, he would wreck it in the morning. "Be tranquil, ladies," he added cheerfully, "you shall be as safely protected under my administration as under that of Mr. Madison." He then bade everybody a polite good-night and headed back to Capitol Hill.

A single sentry was left on guard at the newspaper offices. This lone soldier was the total British occupation force in central Washington that night. The rest of the men of the 3rd Brigade bivouacked on Capitol Hill, while the 2,300 of the 1st and 2nd brigades remained at the edge of the city, watching the flames from the heights just inside the tollgate.

For the capital's scattered population it was a night of sheer terror. The fire dominated everything. It glowed brightly at Baltimore forty miles away, where the citizens gazed in alarm from the rooftops. It hovered over General Winder at Tenleytown, three miles north of Georgetown, as he tried in vain to regroup his shattered army. It rose and fell across the horizon, spurring on Secretaries Armstrong and Campbell as they hurried toward Frederick, Maryland, where the government was to reconvene.

Typical of this chaotic night, none of the other administration leaders was going there. At the moment, they were hopelessly scattered about the Virginia countryside. James Madison, Attorney General Richard Rush, and the rest of the Presidential party rode to Salona, the estate of the Reverend John Maffitt, where Madison now expected to meet his wife. Secretary Monroe went to Wiley's Tavern, near Great Falls. Secretary Jones was with his family and Dolley Madison's entourage, struggling through the clogged roads toward the Salona rendezvous. They finally decided they would never make it and spent the night at Rokeby, the home of Mrs. Madison's friend Mathilda Lee Love. Here, the First Lady sat silently by an open window where she, too, watched the great angry scar in the sky.

Relief finally came from the heavens. Toward dawn one of Washington's patented thunderstorms rumbled in, wetting down the fires and ending the danger that the flames might spread to the whole city.

During the long night of burning no one had gotten to the rather pedestrian brick building that housed the State, War, and Navy departments just west of the executive mansion. The next morning, August 25, a fresh contingent of the British 1st Brigade, followed by some thirty blacks carrying powder and rockets, was assigned to remedy the omission.

As they reached the scene a lone horseman darted out from nowhere. It was John Lewis, erratic grandnephew of the sainted Washington. Long ago, Lewis had run away to sea, suffered impressment by the Royal Navy, and escaped, and ever since he had been burning with vengeance. At last the moment had come. Possibly fortified by a dram or two, he charged the head of the column in a wild, one-man confrontation. He fired his pistol, hit no one, caught a blast of return fire, and fell from his horse mortally wounded.

Now the work could proceed. The Americans had moved most of the current records, but there was still plenty of fuel. Fed by such varied kindling as Secretary Jones's furniture and undistributed copies of the Army's *System of Drum-Beating*, the fire quickly mushroomed through the building.

That finished, the detachment headed back east along F Street. Next on their schedule was a visit to the Patent Office and Post Office, which shared an empty hotel building at Eighth Street. Here they had an unexpected encounter with Dr. William Thornton, the Superintendent of Patents.

Dr. Thornton was one of those universal men, essentially eighteenth century, who aspired to be an expert on everything. Born in the Virgin Islands, he took his medical degree at Aberdeen University, drifted to America, and within a couple of years had submitted the winning design for the U.S. Capitol. Characteristically, he had no architectural training whatsoever. He was obviously Jefferson's kind of man and in 1802 was put in charge of patents. He never took his administrative duties seriously; rather, he used his time to pursue his own catholic interests.

At the moment, he was working on a new kind of violin, which he kept in his room at the Patent Office. He had left it there in his flight the previous evening, but at daylight, when he heard that the British hadn't touched the Patent Office yet, he rushed to the city. He was just in time; the British troops had arrived and were preparing to burn the building. A Major Waters, who seemed to be in charge, told him to go ahead— save the violin and any other private property.

This gave the doctor an inspiration. Turning to Waters, he announced that practically everything in the building was private property. Clearly the course to follow was to take out the few items of public property, burn them in the street, and leave the building alone. Otherwise he could never get out the hundreds of inventors' models that filled the place. Hitting his stride, Thornton dramatically warned that "to burn what would be useful to all mankind would be as barbarous as to burn the Alexandria Library, for which the Turks have been condemned by all enlightened nations."

Thoroughly shaken, Waters said they'd better see his superior, Major Timothy Jones. The major, it turned out, was at the offices of the *National Intelligencer*, carrying out Admiral Cockburn's instructions to wreck the place. When reached, he cheerfully accepted Dr. Thornton's arguments, and the Patent Office was saved.

The *National Intelligencer* was another matter. Cockburn himself was on hand to make sure that place was destroyed. He even helped carry out Gales's reference library, which was burned in back of the building. Then he watched with approval as Jones's men smashed the presses and hurled the type out the windows. "Be sure that all the *c*'s are destroyed," the Admiral joked, "so the rascals can't abuse my name any more."

Gales's home might have gone next but for a quick-witted housekeeper. She closed the shutters and chalked on the front door "For Rent."

Cockburn would have appreciated that. Along with his toughness, he had a sort of zestful joy for combat that al-

lowed plenty of room for tricks, recklessness, improvisation— almost anything except stodginess. Today he was understandably pleased with himself.

As he happily supervised the destruction of the newspaper office he asked a wide-eyed young lady standing at her door, "Were you not prepared to see a savage, a ferocious creature, such as Josey represented me? But you see I am quite harmless; don't be afraid, I will take better care of you than Jemmy did!"

In contrast with Cockburn, General Ross seemed strangely subdued. He never returned to the center of town but spent most of his time either at the camp or at the Ewell house on Capitol Hill, commiserating with the doctor on the hardships of war. Yes, he was sorry he had burned the Library of Congress; no, he would never have burned the President's House had Mrs. Madison been there.

Neither of these officers, however, tolerated looting. Both Ross and Cockburn knew how easy it was for an army to get out of hand in an occupied town. At least seven men were flogged —some for trivial offenses. They took their punishment with the stoicism of Napoleonic veterans, although one man was heard to complain that it was "damn hard, after being in the service eighteen years, that I should be flogged for taking a damn Yankee goose."

In the many encounters between victors and vanquished, the one that both sides thought about most often never came to pass. This was, of course, the union between the black man and the English liberator. The white citizens of Washington had long dreaded the possibility of a slave uprising. Sir Alexander Cochrane, for his part, had long relished the idea of "thousands" of blacks flocking to his colors. Now here the British were, right in the American capital, and nobody came.

The answer went deeper than anyone cared to penetrate: the blacks trusted neither side. There were individual exceptions, of course, but the vast majority wanted no part of it. Now that the British were here, the inclination was to hide rather than rejoice.

And so the hours of tension passed while the work of destruction went on. Lieutenant James Scott led a party of seamen to one of the city's three ropewalks, spread the hemp along the center of the building, poured tar on top, and lit the mixture. The other ropewalks were treated the same way, and in less than half an hour all three were in flames. In a panic the militia on the Virginia side of the Potomac feared a British attack was coming and lit their end of the bridge across the river. Seeing the smoke and commotion and deciding it must mean an American attack, the guard at the British end did the same.

The shimmering August heat grew worse, and great thunderheads were piling up in the northwest when one more British detachment left Capitol Hill around 2 P.M. Consisting of four officers and two hundred men, it marched down Delaware Avenue to Greenleaf's Point, where the Eastern Branch flowed into the Potomac. The Americans had destroyed the fort there, but the magazine remained, and the detachment had orders to get rid of its 150 barrels of powder.

A deep well on the point seemed ideal for the purpose, and the troops began rolling the barrels to the edge and dropping them in. Unknown to everyone, there was not enough water to cover the powder, and the contents of the barrels (plus some of the barrels themselves) soon rose high above the surface.

No one ever knew just how it happened. Some said a soldier accidentally tossed a lighted brand down the well; some said he did it on purpose as the safest way to extinguish it; some said he threw a cigar; some said nobody threw anything: it was the barrels, tumbling down the shaft, that struck sparks off the stone siding. Whatever the cause, the result was the same—an earsplitting explosion that blew well, powder, dirt, buildings, and human beings into a huge, jumbled, mangled mass.

It was worse than any single moment at Bladensburg. Some of the men were blown to pieces, and no one knew exactly how many were killed. Estimates ran from twelve to thirty. The forty-four badly injured were carried back to Capitol Hill, where Ross established a makeshift hospital.

Calm slowly returned to the city, but not the hot, still calm of before. Black clouds to the northwest were rolling closer, muttering with thunder, and flashes of lightning blinked across the sky. It grew steadily darker. A sudden breeze kicked up the dust on Pennsylvania Avenue, and large drops of rain began to fall. Old Washingtonians knew they were in for a really big storm.

But nobody could remember anything like this one—the crashing thunder, the blinding rain, that howling, lashing wind. It plucked Lieutenant Gleig right off his horse. It picked up two British three-pounders as though they were toys. It ripped the roof off the Patent Office, just saved by Dr. Thornton.

Cockburn sat out the storm in the Ewells' dining room, amiably chatting with the doctor. Suddenly, the front door flew open and in stamped four men with a dripping white flag. Led by the Reverend James Muir, they were a "peace" delegation of three clergymen from Alexandria, Virginia. They had battled their way through the storm to explain that their city was completely defenseless—what surrender terms could they expect? It all seemed so anticipatory. Cockburn asked whether Captain James Gordon's squadron was in sight yet, coming up the Potomac. No, it turned out, no one was near; they just wanted to know the terms when their time came.

For once in his life the Admiral was nonplussed. He wasn't used to these people who surrendered without even an enemy in sight. Improvising as best he could, he said that if there was ab-

solutely no resistance, their persons and property would be safe, that the British would take but pay for whatever they needed. With that, he ran out of ideas, and the delegation politely bowed themselves out of the room and back into the storm.

Nor was Alexandria the only place attempting to surrender. The people of Georgetown had been trying for two days. During the evening of the twenty-fourth, Mayor John Peter led a delegation of leading citizens in the first attempt to negotiate terms. They apparently never made contact—they were on the wrong road—but the same group was at it again bright and early on the twenty-fifth. This time they reached Ross and offered to give up the town if only the British would spare their houses.

The General turned out to be a surprisingly good bluffer. He let them believe he was interested, but actually he had no intention of going farther west. There were rumors that the American Army had rallied on the heights above Georgetown, and he certainly didn't want to get trapped.

In fact, General Ross was determined to head back to the fleet right away. The explosion at Greenleaf's Point had wiped out some of his best men; the storm had torn his organization to shreds. Now there were reports of American reinforcements coming on, twelve thousand men massed for a great counterattack. His pickets said they could even see weapons glittering on the heights above the Potomac. As for himself, he had already accomplished more than he ever hoped. More than he dreamed. Why stretch his luck?

As evening approached, staff officers quietly alerted the various unit commanders to be ready to fall back after dark. Secrecy was all-important. Not a word to the men or the people of the town. Where the sudden bustle of activity required some explanation, the inhabitants were fed vague, misleading rumors: there were hints of a move on Annapolis, on Georgetown.

The forty-four badly injured at Greenleaf's Point couldn't be moved, and nothing was more upsetting to General Ross. Dr. Ewell assured Ross that Americans were a humane people —"of the same origin as yourself"—and that he personally would look after the men left behind.

At dusk the campfires blazed brightly on Capitol Hill and at the larger encampment on the edge of the city. Occasional figures, silhouetted or caught in the flickering light, hovered about doing ordinary chores. It was, of course, the oldest of *ruses de guerre*. While a handful of men played out a charade, the great mass of the army stole away in the night. Falling in at 8 P.M., the 3rd Brigade led the way, then the 2nd, then the 1st, silently marching out Maryland Avenue, the exact way they had entered twenty-four hours ago.

For five days, town by town, they retraced their steps to the fleet. Not a shot was fired at them all the way; not a bridge destroyed nor a tree chopped down to check their progress. They had seen few enemy troops on the way in; they saw none on the way out.

In a few incredible days the British force had marched fifty miles into the enemy's country, captured his capital, burned the public buildings, and gotten back safely to their ships.

Rear Admiral George Cockburn (pronounced Coburn), in full dress uniform complete with epaulets and spurs, is grandly portrayed before the flaming ruins of Washington. The building at far right appears to be the Capitol. I. J. Hall, the painter of this noble portrait, was obviously English.

Among the retiring British troops, there were a few stragglers who stayed behind in the Maryland countryside to loot. A group of Americans, largely led by Dr. William Beanes, the elderly patriarch of Upper Marlboro whose house had served as Ross's headquarters on his way to Washington, captured and jailed some of these stragglers. One man escaped and brought word to the fleet. General Ross, furious at what he considered a breach of faith on his former host's part, sent back a force to arrest Beanes and his police party. The other Americans were soon released, but Beanes was thrown in the brig of the flagship Tonnant.

No one knew what the British planned to do next. Alexandria rushed to surrender to Captain Gordon when his squadron, still sailing up the Potomac toward Washington, came into sight. Americans were shamed, angry, and bitter as the news of the burning of the capital spread. Every city in the area feared that its turn was next.

Meanwhile, the British, regrouping their forces and waiting for Gordon to return, were making plans. Hatred of Baltimore, that "nest of pirates," was strong, and Cockburn wanted to attack that city immediately. Cochrane and Ross, however, were more cautious. They finally decided to regroup, rest the force at Rhode Island, and return to Baltimore in October. Knowing none of this, the cities along the seaboard continued their frantic preparations.

PART **2**

TRIUMPH
AT
BALTIMORE

Boasting a population of over forty-five thousand, Baltimore was the third-biggest city in the Union—a target of obvious importance. Its bulging warehouses and crowded waterfront invited the closest attention of the prize-conscious British leaders. Its record of harassing the enemy was unparalleled—over five hundred British ships captured or sent to the bottom by Baltimore privateers.

And it had a reputation to go with its record. No city had done more to fan the war fever. In one anti-Federalist riot a crowd even killed a distinguished Revolutionary leader and maimed the venerated Richard Henry Lee, seemingly just because they wanted peace. "Mobtown" was the gentlest epithet applied by the British press.

Yet at the moment, brawling, bellicose Baltimore was anything but warlike. As the shattered remnants of Brigadier General Tobias Stansbury's and Colonel Joseph Sterett's militia tumbled in from Bladensburg, a wave of defeatism swept the city. "You may be sure this is the most awful moment of my life," one of the stunned inhabitants, David Winchester, wrote a relative in Tennessee. "Not because, if the place is defended, I shall put my life at hazard in common with my fellow citizens, but because I am positively sure we shall not succeed."

Few even contemplated a defense. "I think the only way to save the town and state will be to capitulate," wrote Private Henry Fulford, back home from his harrowing day at Bladensburg. "We shall have to receive the British without opposition

and make the best terms we can," echoed a local shipowner in a letter to New York. He added that he had to close now; he was off to scuttle his own vessel in the harbor.

Baltimore's postmaster hastily made plans to shift the mails out of town. The banks began moving their specie to York, Pennsylvania. Many members of the Committee of Vigilance and Safety—just formed to organize the city's defense—seemed more interested in arranging capitulation than resistance. One of the committee's most prominent members, John Eager Howard, desperately tried to stem the tide. Pointing out that he had four sons in the field and as much property as anyone, he said he would rather see his sons killed and his property in ashes than surrender and disgrace the country.

On August 25, Brigadier General John Stricker, command-

ing Baltimore's militia, stalked into the council chamber where the Committee of Vigilance and Safety was meeting. With him came Captain Oliver Hazard Perry, in town to take over the new frigate *Java;* Captain Robert T. Spence, another senior Naval officer; and Major George Armistead, commanding the regulars at Fort McHenry, which guarded the entrance to Baltimore's harbor.

Together they called for all-out resistance. Burying the usual service rivalries, they also urged that a single overall commander be appointed for the city's defenses. The man they wanted was Major General Samuel Smith, commanding the 3rd Division of Maryland militia, the main body of troops in the area. The committee agreed, and Smith accepted the appointment subject to one condition: he wanted Governor Levin

the *BALTIMOREANS.*

American war cartoonists in 1814 were apparently just as verbose as their British counterparts. (See page 51.) This busy caricature shows John Bull bringing up the rear of the British retreat at Baltimore. Groaning about "Defeat and Disgrace," he is being prodded rudely by a bayonet.

Winder's sanction, including whatever extended powers might be necessary to do the job.

That condition told a lot about Sam Smith, as he was universally known. After twenty years in Congress—first as representative, now as senator—he knew all the pressure points of the body politic. Military authority from some citizens' committee didn't mean much, but from the governor himself—that was different. Especially if, as here, the governor also happened to be the uncle of Brigadier General Winder, the Regular Army officer commanding the District. A clash of authority seemed likely, and Smith wanted to cover himself.

This kind of shrewdness, coupled with hard-driving ambition, sound judgment, and a freewheeling style, had carried Sam Smith a long way. Born in Pennsylvania, he grew up in Baltimore, the strong-willed son of a wealthy merchant. In the Revolution he organized a company, joined George Washington, and shared the trials of Long Island, White Plains, Brandywine, Monmouth. For the defense of Fort Mifflin he got a sword and a vote of thanks from Congress. Yet even in those dark days he still had a streak of personal ambition that set him aside from the rest of that band of heroes. He somehow got back to Baltimore every winter for recruiting and business, and long before the war was over he resigned his commission and went home to make money.

He prospered mightily—in iron, shipping, banking, land, everything he touched—and was soon in politics, too. Elected to Congress in 1792, he was not so much a legislator as a manipulator.

Now, at sixty-two, he was as shrewd, tough, and ambitious as ever. Maybe not the ideal man for the long winter at Valley Forge, but for the short haul no one had more drive or commanded more respect. Significantly, three of the leaders who proposed him were regulars, who traditionally hated to serve under a militia officer. This time they had no qualms, for here was a man who could get things done.

So an express galloped off to Annapolis, and by the twenty-sixth he was back with the governor's blessing. It proved a masterpiece of evasion, for, apart from avuncular considerations, Levin Winder was faced with a most delicate problem. Normally, General Winder, a regular, outranked Smith, a militia officer. But if called into federal service, Smith, a major general, outranked Winder, a brigadier. The hitch was that nobody had called Smith into federal service. Under the Presidential order of last July, General Winder had the authority but never exercised it. On the other hand, Governor Winder had no authority in such matters at all. The governor solved the problem by simply implying that Smith had been called into federal service: "By the requisition of the President of the United States of the 4th of July last, one Major General is required of this state. In conformity to which, you have been selected."

That was good enough for Sam Smith. "The endorsed copy of a letter from His Excellency Governor Winder was received by me this day, and I have in consequence assumed the command agreeably to my rank," he quickly wrote General Winder, who was hurrying toward Baltimore to organize the city's defense himself. And if that didn't get across the point, the rest of Smith's message showed the tone of command already creeping into his pen: "Do me the favor to send me in-

formation by the dragoon of your situation, the number of troops with you. We want the tents and equipage of Stansbury's Brigade. . . ."

General Winder was thunderstruck. Arriving in Baltimore at 3 A.M. on the twenty-seventh, he rested a few sleepless hours, then went to see Smith. It was a stormy session: Winder protesting that he still had command, that the governor had no power to name anybody; Smith insisting he was now in charge and expected to give the orders. In the end Winder got nowhere, but whatever his merits as a general, he was too decent a man—too good a patriot—to sulk or walk out. Swallowing his pride, he said he'd do whatever Smith asked until the issue could be settled by Washington.

"General Winder has in a manner much to his honor I conceive, consented to waive his pretentions to rank for the present," Commodore John Rodgers wrote approvingly to Secretary of the Navy Jones later that day. Rodgers had been present during the whole confrontation, and as a regular himself he agreed with Winder's legal position. But he had been in Baltimore since the night of the twenty-fifth, had seen the panic firsthand, and knew how desperately a strong leader was needed. Somehow he managed to give his sympathy to Winder and his support to Smith without alienating either of those sensitive warriors.

He himself was a tower of strength these trying days. As senior officer of the U.S. Navy, his presence alone gave new heart to Baltimore, while his three hundred seamen from Philadelphia were the first tangible evidence that help was on the way. By combining them with the five hundred flotilla men in town—plus Captain David Porter's force, soon down from New York—Rodgers put together a makeshift "brigade," which he made as conspicuous as possible.

But there was so much to be done. The best of the Maryland militia had been at Bladensburg, and on the twenty-seventh they were still hopelessly scattered. When Sam Smith issued a call to Stansbury's men to report, only six hundred of the approximately 2,200 who had served at Bladensburg showed up. His somewhat imperious order telling Winder to bring on Stansbury's tents and equipage was ludicrous—everything was still lost in Virginia. Even Sterett's elite 5th Regiment seemed to have vanished. Want ads blossomed in the *Patriot and Evening Advertiser* pleading for William Pinkney's Riflemen and the American Artilleryists routed at Bladensburg to reassemble. An even more revealing ad summoned to the courthouse "elderly men, who are able to carry a firelock, and willing to render a last service to their country."

It was a situation made for Sam Smith, and every Baltimorean soon knew it. On the twenty-seventh the citizens were told to collect all the wheelbarrows, pickaxes, and shovels they could find. On the twenty-eighth they started digging. A line of fortifications gradually took shape along the eastern edge of the city—the side most exposed to a British landing.

Smith seemed everywhere, and into everything at once. He quickly proved a dynamo of energy and a volcano of temper.

This 1816 portrait of Sam Smith, painted by Rembrandt Peale, shows the forceful, tactless hero of Baltimore in a calm and statesmanlike mood.
THE PEALE MUSEUM, BALTIMORE

On August 29 the Pennsylvania and Virginia militia began coming in; he wanted no more "Bladensburg Races" and drilled them mercilessly from reveille to 7 P.M. On August 30 Commodore Rodgers and the Naval contingent left briefly on a futile attempt to stop the British squadron on the Potomac; Smith fumed and stormed, urged Rodgers to come back "immy." On August 31 Quartermaster Paul Bentalou announced he had no money and could get none from the War Department. Smith charged over to the Committee of Vigilance and Safety and engineered an immediate loan of a hundred thousand dollars from the Baltimore banks.

That same day he scored an especially characteristic stroke when the War Department ordered five 18-pounders at Fort McHenry to be transferred to Washington. "The guns belong to the U.S.," he wrote the Committee of Vigilance and Safety, "but the carriages are the property of the City. I have therefore not conceived myself at liberty to deliver them without the consent of your Committee. I consider these guns as indispensable. . . ." The committee took the cue and told the War Department that it could have the guns but not the carriages. That way, they were of very little use to anybody, and Washington quietly capitulated.

On September 1 the units crowding into town began battling over the few available wagons—Smith intervened and divided them up: one wagon for every one hundred men. Arbitrary, but it worked. On September 2 the troops were running out of bread because all the bakers were drilling. Again Smith stepped in, released the bakers from service, told the contractors to hire them and start making biscuits. On September 3 military traffic ground to a halt; the streets were clogged with caissons, carts, wagons of every sort. Once again Smith exploded into action, ordering a bridge of scows across the inner harbor. It looked a little visionary, but in two days thirty scows were in place and the bridge operating.

Sam Smith was not a man to delegate authority, and his headaches came in all sizes. One minute he was straightening out the different countersigns used by the sentries, the next he was trying to dispose of forty head of surplus cattle brought along by a Virginia brigade.

In the hubbub around headquarters it sometimes seemed as if nothing got done, but actually a great transformation was taking place. A week ago Hampstead Hill was a placid green rise to the east of town; now the dirt was flying. "They are throwing up entrenchments all around the city," an unidentified young lady wrote her brother in New York, who passed her letter on to the *Evening Post*. "White and black are all at work together. You'll see a master and his slave digging side by side. There is no distinction whatsoever."

The citizens worked in relays, depending on the ward where they lived. They reported at 6 A.M. and toiled till dark. Everybody joined in. When twelve-year-old Sam W. Smith, the General's nephew, disappeared from home, the family knew just where to find him—out on Hampstead Hill, digging away with the rest.

A less visible but equally important change was the sudden flow of money for defense. A week ago the talk was of paying ransom; now it was of buying guns, tents, provisions, forage. Washington had said it had no cash; very well, the Baltimoreans declared, they would finance their own needs. With just a little prodding from Sam Smith, the local banks ultimately advanced $663,000 for the cause. Less spectacular, but more poignant, were the hundreds of donations showered on the town by its loyal citizens. And where cash was impractical, the people came through with goods and services. The variety was a nightmare to the city comptroller: Luke and William Enson, three thousand bricks; Dr. Henry Karl, two bundles of lint; C. White & Sons, five barrels of whiskey; "A Citizen," three tons of hay.

But the biggest change of all was the mass of volunteers pouring in from every direction. A week ago Baltimore lay wide open; now troops—from Maryland, from Virginia, from Pennsylvania—seemed to fill every inch of space. By September 4 Quartermaster Bentalou estimated there were fifteen thousand men on hand. That day General Thomas Forman, the commander of Maryland's 1st Brigade, enthusiastically wrote his wife, "We have assembled seven generals: Smith, Winder, Stricker, and Stansbury of Baltimore; Douglass and Singleton of Virginia; and your humble servant. This morning all the general officers with their aides and brigade majors assembled at 6 o'clock to view the grounds and country surrounding Baltimore. The parade was splendid and interesting. . . ."

All seemed in perfect harmony as this array of braid and cocked hats swung by the serried ranks, but beneath the surface General Winder still seethed at the thought of being just one of seven. He had been appointed by the President of the United States in person to command the 10th Military District—which certainly included Baltimore—yet this fractious militia officer had brazenly seized control, and apparently nothing could be done about it. And worse was to follow. When Winder got his formal assignment from Smith on September 5, he found his job was to defend the Ferry Branch of the Patapsco. This backwater was the western anchor of the city's defense line, yet it was to the east that Baltimore's fate would most likely be decided. Clearly he was on the shelf.

"After the candour which I have uniformly evinced toward you," the General wrote Smith on the sixth, "I cannot for a moment suppose that in the assignment of my command and station any other motive than that of a just regard to my rank and other circumstances influenced you, and yet I cannot but believe that in a review of the arrangement you have made you will be satisfied that it is unjust as relates to my rank and situation and in derogation from the ordinary principles of military service."

Smith never even answered. Tact was not one of his high points. In fact, while Winder was pouring out his heart Smith was absorbed in his fortifications.

But what, during these frenzied days, was the enemy doing? Along with his other precautions, Sam Smith had stationed lookouts along the Chesapeake, but they had little to report. From the Goodwin house near the tip of North Point, day after day Major Josiah Green sent back a laconic "There is nothing

of the enemy below." From the dome of the State House at Annapolis, Major William Barney (the Commodore's son) could only say, "There is nothing in sight." Occasionally Governor Winder himself would clamber up the creaking ladder and take a turn with the glass. But the eyes of the statesman were no sharper than any others in catching a sign of the next British move.

While Sam Smith was goading Baltimore into preparedness, Dr. Beanes's friends were working on a plan to win his release. Francis Scott Key got President Madison's permission to sail out to the British fleet under a flag of truce to plead for the distinguished doctor's freedom. With him went John S. Skinner, the American prisoner-of-war exchange agent, who had dealt with the British before. Wisely, they took also a packet of letters from the British wounded being cared for in Washington, attesting to the humane treatment they were receiving. When Key and Skinner finally reached Ross aboard the Tonnant *on September 7, these letters proved more important than any legal arguments. Ross agreed to release Dr. Beanes.*

That same day, however, the British plans had changed—probably because of intelligence just received—and the decision had been made to attack Baltimore as soon as Captain Gordon returned. Under the circumstances Dr. Beanes and his rescuers were to be detained, and they were transferred to the frigate Surprize.

On September 9, Gordon having successfully descended the Potomac, the reassembled fleet was on its way. On the tenth, as the ships swept up the Chesapeake, Annapolis made panicky plans to surrender. But the fleet sailed right past the town. By evening a final message went out from Annapolis to Baltimore: fifty ships were heading north, up Chesapeake Bay, under a full press of canvas.

By September 10 Baltimore was ready. Sam Smith had 16,391 men packed into a network of land and water defenses covering the eastern and southern approaches to the city. From the Bel Air Road northeast of town a line of earthworks curved south past the hospital, along the brow of Hampstead Hill, and down to the Sugar House at the edge of the harbor. Overall, the line boasted sixty-two guns supported by over ten thousand troops. Most of them were militia.

At the harbor Sam Smith's problem was complicated by the nature of local geography. Lying twelve miles up the Patapsco River from Chesapeake Bay, Baltimore could be easily reached by the lighter British warships. Approaching the city, moreover, the river split at Whetstone Point into two branches, and both had to be considered in planning defense. The right-hand fork, coming in from the Bay, was called the Northwest Branch, and it led straight to the main waterfront. The other fork—the Ferry Branch—curved off to the west, but at Ridgely's Cove it still came within a mile of the town.

Sam Smith began by sealing off the Northwest Branch at its mouth. There was already a boom here, running from a projec-

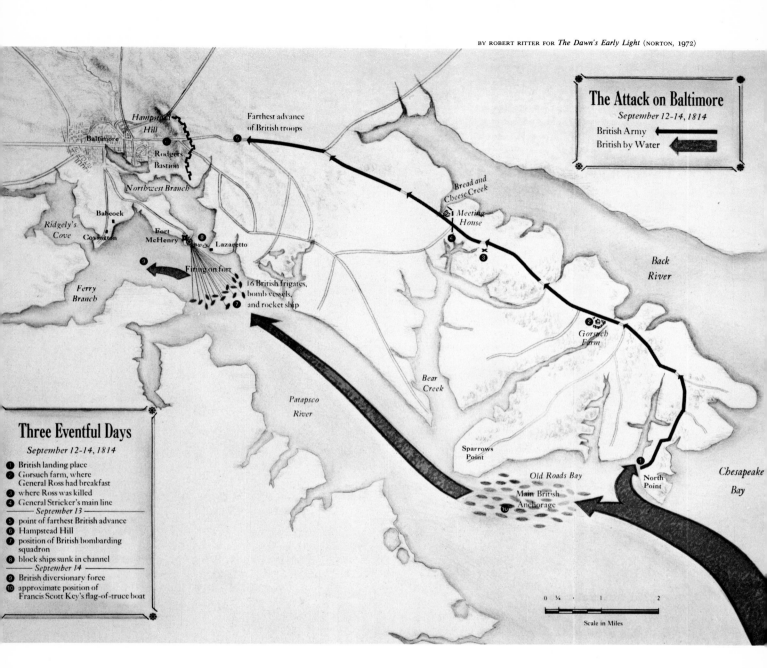

BY ROBERT RITTER FOR *The Dawn's Early Light* (NORTON, 1972)

The Attack on Baltimore

September 12-14, 1814

British Army ⬅

British by Water ⬅

Three Eventful Days

September 12-14, 1814

1. British landing place
2. Gorsuch farm, where General Ross had breakfast
3. where Ross was killed
4. General Stricker's main line
   — *September 13* —
5. point of farthest British advance
6. Hampstead Hill
7. position of British bombarding squadron
8. block ships sunk in channel
   — *September 14* —
9. British diversionary force
10. approximate position of Francis Scott Key's flag-of-truce boat

0 ¼ · 1 · 2

Scale in Miles

tion called the Lazaretto to Whetstone Point, but it looked flimsy, so Smith backed it up with a line of barges bristling with cannon. At the Lazaretto itself he added a three-gun battery manned by some of Barney's flotilla men.

At Whetstone Point, the other anchor of the barrier, Smith could count on the only permanent fixture in the whole defense system—picturesque, star-shaped Fort McHenry. Begun during the Revolution and improved from time to time, it was there to defend both the Northwest Branch to the east and the Ferry Branch to the west. Its red brick masonry had a sturdy, spunky look that endeared itself to Baltimoreans, but how good it really was nobody knew.

Sam Smith was taking no chances. Starting even before the present emergency, he had wangled, argued, begged, threat-

ened, used all his driving energy to strengthen the place. He had installed fifteen 36-pounders from the *Eole*, a French warship stranded in the harbor, built a furnace for heating shot, and added new outworks at the edge of the river. Now he extended the parapet and the harbor boom around the tip of Whetstone Point and beefed up Major Armistead's 250-man garrison with hundreds of regulars, flotilla men, Sea Fencibles, militiamen, and Judge Joseph H. Nicholson's Artillery Fencibles, a company of gentlemen volunteers who had their own hot coffee especially brought out from the city every morning. By September 10 at least fifty-seven guns and about a thousand men were crammed into the little fort.

Sam Smith's labors went on—so effectively that Baltimore's problem swung from a lack of preparation to a surfeit of confidence. The 3rd Brigade dispensed with its morning drills. General Forman expected his brigade would be discharged by September 13 or 14—"then home with all speed to see my darling wife."

Even stern, conscientious Commodore Rodgers was not immune. Writing a friend in Philadelphia on the ninth, he observed that Baltimore "now has nothing to fear even should the enemy make his appearance tomorrow. It is understood, however, that he has descended the Bay, and whatever might have been his intentions, that he will not now attempt an attack on this place. . . . I hope to leave here in two or three days for Philadelphia, as I begin to feel tired of playing the soldier."

Perhaps too many others felt the same way—explaining the lack of excitement Saturday night, September 10, when reports of ship sightings began arriving from Annapolis. General Winder sent a hurry call for cartridge boxes. Judge Nicholson's Fencibles, in town for the weekend, hastily reassembled to march back to Fort McHenry. But on the whole, Baltimore spent a quiet, uneventful Saturday night.

Sunday the eleventh began quietly, too. While Sam Smith and Commodore Rodgers huddled over a scheme to sink block-ships in the Northwest Branch, most of Baltimore went to church as usual. At the Wilkes Street Methodist Church, some soldiers stacked their arms outside the door and joined the congregation.

Suddenly, toward 1:30 P.M., the quiet of the Sabbath was shattered by the sound of three shots fired from cannon on the courthouse green. As the Wilkes Street Methodists buzzed with excitement and the troops scrambled for the door, the minister quickly closed his Bible. "My brethren and friends," he announced, "the alarm guns have just fired. The British are approaching and commending you to God and the word of His Grace, I pronounce the benediction, and may the God of battles accompany you."

At the Light Street Methodist Church, the Reverend John Gruber was even more to the point: "May the Lord bless King George, convert him, and take him to heaven, as we want no more of him."

Outside, it was bedlam. Troops were racing to their positions; wagons bulging with women, children, and furniture rattled north on Charles Street, heading out of town. Breasting the stream of refugees, Private Mendes I. Cohen, an eighteen-year-old recruit, hurried to get back to his post at Fort McHenry. Late as he was, he couldn't help pausing at the observation station on Federal Hill. In the shimmering haze twelve miles down the Patapsco, he could make out the whole British fleet standing into North Point.

This was just the way Sam Smith thought it would be. He was always sure the biggest danger lay to the east, in a British landing on the jagged peninsula that jutted into the Bay between the Patapsco and Back rivers, ending at North Point. Now he ordered Brigadier General John Stricker to take his City Brigade, totalling some 3,200 men, and head for North Point at once.

Stricker was the natural choice for this assignment. A Revolutionary War veteran slightly younger than Smith, he had occasionally served under the commanding general in militia operations and seemed to be one of the few officers who could get along with the old man. His City Brigade was also well cho-

sen. These troops came from Baltimore, were highly motivated, and included most of the 5th Regiment and Pinkney's Riflemen, who were all veterans of Bladensburg. While this was not entirely a recommendation, nevertheless there was something to be said for experience, and the 5th had at least made a brief stand.

At 3 P.M. they fell in and headed east on Baltimore Street. Led by fife and drum, they presented the usual mixture of dashing uniforms and civilian dress. They ranged from military dandies like Captain Aaron Levering's Independent Blues, with their stylish red cuffs and white crossbelts, to rank amateurs like Private John Smith of the Union Volunteers. He soon lost his knapsack containing a "swan's down vest, a pair of nankeen pantaloons, a linen shirt, and striped cravat." Tramping down Baltimore Street, they presented less a picture of martial splendor than of earnest endeavor. Yet there was something poignant about them, too, and as they passed the house of the Reverend John Glendy he blessed them and prayed for their safety and success.

Unlike Saturday, Sunday was a restless night at Baltimore. By sunset the lookouts on Federal Hill had counted forty-seven to fifty British sail, including ten transports "all within the bar." At the Lazaretto, Lieutenant Solomon Rutter went over the night signals he had just worked out with Major Armistead across the barricaded river at Fort McHenry: "Enemy in sight or approaching—one gun, one false fire, one blue light, repeated until answered."

Armistead himself was worn to the bone. Professionally, there was the loneliness of command—he and apparently he alone knew that Fort McHenry's magazine was not bomb-proof. Personally, there was an aching concern for his wife Louisa. He had sent her off to safety at Gettysburg, but she was expecting a baby and he continued to worry. Friday night he dreamed she had presented him with a son; tonight there was no time to dream, or even to sleep.

Twelve miles east of Fort McHenry on the sloop *Fairy*, General Ross and Admiral Cockburn were putting the final touches on their landing plan. Cockburn had wanted to lead the barges and cutters up the Patapsco and storm Fort McHenry, but he had been overruled in favor of a two-pronged attack. Now the troops would go ashore at North Point and advance up the peninsula to assail Baltimore by land, while the bomb vessels, a rocket ship, and the frigates would advance up the river to strike the city by water.

Once taken, there would be no mercy. A new letter had arrived from the British governor in Canada, Sir George Prevost, telling of fresh atrocities by the Americans, and Admiral Cochrane was determined to retaliate on Baltimore. As he always said, you had to treat these people like spaniels. The troops were appropriately equipped for serious business. The ammunition allotment was increased from sixty to eighty rounds per man, and all frills were to be left behind. Lieutenant Gleig of

His Majesty's 85th Foot—always the officer and gentleman—resigned himself to sharing a hairbrush with another man.

Quite aware of these harsh plans, John Skinner and Francis Scott Key waited out the night back on their own flag-of-truce boat. They had been transferred to her during the day—either because, as Key later recalled, Cochrane needed the *Surprize* himself as a shallow-draft flagship or because, as Skinner told it, he had demanded that they suffer through the attack at least on a vessel flying their own colors. In any event, they weren't yet free to leave. When Skinner had broached this possibility during the afternoon, Cochrane had simply smiled and said, "Ah, Mr. Skinner, after discussing so freely our preparation and plans, you could hardly expect us to let you go on shore in advance of us."

They had, nevertheless, persuaded General Ross to release Dr. Beanes from confinement. The old gentleman immediately joined them, and now the three Americans wondered and waited together—still the unwilling guests of this hostile armada lying quietly under the stars.

At 2 A.M. on the twelfth the silent ships came suddenly to life. A gun brig moved close inshore, prepared to rake the beach if any Americans appeared. Barges and cutters swarmed around the transports, taking off the troops. At 3 A.M. the whole collection of small craft began moving toward the shore. By six thirty the columns were formed, ready for marching. Leading them all was General Robert Ross, and by his side was the gusty, rambunctious figure of Rear Admiral George Cockburn. At 7 A.M. the bugles sounded, and the British force—now 4,700 strong—started for Baltimore.

Ross knew that the American force defending North Point was large, but he also knew the troops were mostly militiamen, and he didn't care, he said, "if it rains militia." But before the two approaching forces ever made full contact, Ross was killed, shot by an American advance party; no one has ever known for certain who fired the fateful shot.

Colonel Arthur Brooke, the second-ranking officer in the army, assumed command. The two forces met at a narrow neck of land where General John Stricker, the American commander, had arranged his defense line. The battle raged for more than two hours, with the Americans pushed back but not routed. They finally regrouped and camped for the night back near Sam Smith's earthworks. Brooke, inexperienced and uncertain, didn't pursue but camped also. American casualties were 163 killed and wounded; the British had three hundred casualties. The attackers had advanced less than a mile along the route to Baltimore.

On the Patapsco, Admiral Cochrane was making greater progress in carrying out his part of the two-pronged advance. After landing the last of the troops and supplies at North Point, he shifted his flag to the *Surprize* and at 1:30 P.M. ordered the frigates and bomb vessels to head upstream for Baltimore. As yet he knew nothing of Ross's death or the change in command, but he could plainly hear the gunfire ashore, and he struggled to get his ships in position to support the advancing army.

It was a backbreaking job. The Patapsco was not only shallow, but full of unexpected shoals, and the squadron had only two or three pilots who knew the water. The *Seahorse* went ahead to feel the way, but she ran aground almost immediately. For nearly four hours she was either stuck or warping slowly through the mud.

At three thirty the *Surprize* finally anchored at a point about five miles below Fort McHenry. Here she was joined by the *Severn*, flying Cockburn's flag, and the other frigates and brigs. The five bomb vessels and the rocket ship *Erebus* continued creeping closer until they anchored only two and a half miles from the fort.

No one knew how the Americans might react, but Cochrane was taking no chances. He ordered every ship to ready grappling hooks in case the enemy tried fire vessels, as they had on the Potomac. Torpedoes were always a menace, although the Admiral considered them outlawed by the rules of war. He issued careful instructions on towing them clear of endangered craft. Sets of passwords and countersigns were distributed for use in the night.

Sweeping his glass along the shoreline, Cochrane discovered one defense measure he didn't know how to counter. The Americans were busy sinking blockships across the mouth of the Northwest Branch. These would effectively keep him from storming the inner harbor, either to bombard the town or to carry off the prize goods he thought about so much. There was no alternative but to capture Fort McHenry first.

Examining the earthworks on Hampstead Hill, Cochrane felt more encouraged. The defense line swarmed with people and ran right to the water's edge, but it didn't seem to extend very far back into the country. "I think it may be completely turned without the necessity of taking it in front," he wrote that afternoon in a letter addressed to General Ross. He also took the opportunity to outline his own plans: "At daylight we shall place the Bombs and barges to bombard the fort. You will find them over upon the eastern shore, as the enemy have forts upon the western side which it is not necessary to encounter."

At 7:30 P.M. the letter was returned unopened together with the shattering news that Ross was dead.

Cochrane immediately forwarded it to Colonel Brooke, adding some observations that he thought might be useful to the army's new leader. His main concern was that Brooke might be too easy on Baltimore. Ross had been so soft at Washington—all that nonsense about respecting private property—that this new man must be set straight right away:

It is proper for me to mention to you that a system of retaliation was to be proceeded upon in consequence of the barbarities committed in Canada—and if General Ross had seen the second letter from Sir George Prevost he would have destroyed Washington and Georgetown. . . .

So there would be no leniency this time. "I do not like to contemplate scenes of blood and destruction," Cochrane's flag captain, the normally placid Rear Admiral Edward Codrington, wrote to his wife that evening, "but my heart is deeply interested in the coercion of these Baltimore heroes, who are perhaps the most inveterate against us of all the Yankees, and I hope they will be chastized even until they excite my pity, by which time they will be sufficiently humbled."

Baltimore sensed its crisis was at hand. Commodore Rodgers hoped sinking the blockships would tighten the barrier across the Northwest Branch. Until now the merchants of Baltimore had not taken kindly to this idea—they couldn't see the logic of sinking their fortunes to save them—but today, with the British on the doorstep, the mood was different. Down went John Donnell's handsome ship *Chesapeake*, John Craig's brig *Father and Son*, Elie Clagett's schooner *Scudder*—twenty-four vessels altogether. Ultimately, the barrier was extended across the Ferry Branch, too, although there was no time for that just now. As always, Sam Smith looked to the east; the west could take care of itself.

General Winder knew it all too well. For a whole week he had seen his western command neglected or nibbled away. Now a new order came from Smith to send his cavalry to Colonel Nicholas Ruxton Moore, operating east of the town. Winder of course complied but sent at the same time a last, despairing note to headquarters: "This has finally robbed my command of its only means of availing itself of favorable opportunities of annoying the enemy. . . . In fine, I am now fairly destitute of every means by which I can render my command honorable to them or myself as essentially useful to the country, unless by mere accident."

As usual, Sam Smith was too busy to answer, nor did anyone else have time to worry about the ruffled feelings of a forgotten general this hectic afternoon. Around 4 P.M. word spread that General Stricker, commanding the American forces on North Point, was beaten—was falling back—and the whole city plunged into a frantic, last-second rush of preparation. The Committee of Vigilance and Safety ordered all lights out tonight—no point in giving the British gunners a mark to shoot at. Nervous citizens reread the morning *Telegraph*'s instructions on handling incendiaries. "Should Congreve rockets be thrown into the city," the paper advised its apparently well-heeled readers, "we should recommend to every house-keeper to have a servant ready with buckets filled with water to extinguish the flames."

At Fort McHenry, Major Armistead studied the ominous line of British ships lying just out of range. The gun ports were open; small craft were clustered along the sides. "From the number of barges and the known situation of the enemy," he wrote Sam Smith at 4:30, "I have not a doubt but that an assault will be made this night upon the Fort."

At the Lazaretto across the channel, Lieutenant Solomon Rutter worried about British trickery. To guard against a surprise blow, he and Armistead quickly worked out a set of challenges for the night. The password would be "William," the answer "Eutaw."

Such precautions were wise and necessary, but at a time like this a man could also use a little inspiration. The defenders of Fort McHenry got theirs from a huge American flag that flew from a pole just inside the parade ground. Measuring thirty by forty-two feet, it seemed to dominate not only the fort but the outlying strong points and even the defenses on Hampstead Hill. Needless to say, it could also be seen by the newly arrived visitors from Britain.

That was just the way Major Armistead wanted it. During the invasion scare in the summer of 1813 he had written Sam Smith, "We, Sir, are ready at Fort McHenry to defend Baltimore against invading by the enemy. That is to say, we are ready except that we have no suitable ensign to display over the Star Fort, and it is my desire to have a flag so large that the British will have no difficulty in seeing it from a distance."

He had gotten his wish. Some time that summer a committee of high-ranking officers had called on Mary Young Pickersgill, a widow who normally specialized in making house flags for Baltimore's far-flung merchant ships. They had explained their needs, and Mrs. Pickersgill had accepted the order.

Recruiting her thirteen-year-old daughter Caroline to help, she had spent the next several weeks cutting and measuring her bolts of cloth—fifteen white stars, each two feet from point to point, eight red stripes and seven white, each two feet broad. Altogether she had used some four hundred yards of bunting.

Then had come the job of piecing it together. Even the big upstairs bedroom in the Pickersgill house wasn't large enough, so on an inspiration she had borrowed the use of the malthouse in Brown's brewery. Here she and Caroline had continued working—often by candlelight—sewing and basting the colors together.

That August the flag had been delivered at a cost—meticulously calculated by Mrs. Pickersgill—of exactly $405.90. For a year it hadn't been needed, but on this hot, dangerous evening of September 12, 1814, it blazed in the sunset—not an icon of might and power, but rather an expression of earnest purpose, a mark of defiance flown by a small, young, and not always wise country about to take its stand against the strongest nation in the world.

The next morning, Major Armistead's big flag was snapping in a damp, easterly breeze as the British bomb vessel *Volcano* weighed anchor at 5 A.M. and began edging toward Fort McHenry. Close behind came another "bomb," the *Meteor*, and the rocket ship *Erebus*. Also tagging along was the *Cockchafer*, a pugnacious little schooner that always seemed in the middle of things. Later they were joined by three more bombs—the *Terror*, *Devastation*, and *Aetna*—while the frigates and sloops moved up to lend support.

At six thirty the *Volcano* came to, and Captain David Price fired a couple of shots to check the range. Not close enough. The bombs and rocket ship crept on—now less than two miles away—but even before they were in position to fire, the perky *Cockchafer* let loose a broadside at the star-shaped ramparts.

At seven the *Meteor* opened up. Then one by one the other bombs and the *Erebus* joined in, while the *Cockchafer* continued banging away. The guns of the fort roared back, firing erratically but now within range. "The enemy shot falling short and over us," coolly noted the keeper of the *Meteor*'s log.

At 8:40 a cannonball ripped through the mainsail of the *Cockchafer*, and Admiral Cochrane decided to play it a little safer. Shortly after nine he pulled the squadron back to a point slightly over two miles from the fort. This meant sacrificing the firepower of the frigates and the *Erebus*, but that was why he had brought the bombs along.

Compared to the stately frigates and ships of the line, these ungainly vessels weren't much to look at—the *Aetna*, for instance, was a stubby 102 feet long. Nor was service in them fashionable. They fired shells that burst—a bit unsporting, that—and their operation was left largely to the Royal Marine Artillery, who didn't seem to mind. Nevertheless, they were useful and in many ways remarkable ships. Armed principally with two guns—a ten- and a thirteen-inch mortar—they fired huge bombshells that weighed over two hundred pounds and carried up to 4,200 yards—well over two miles.

It took enormous force to do that, and this in turn put enormous strain on the ships every time the mortars were fired. A complicated system of beams and springs was designed to cushion the blow, but even so the jar was terrific. It rattled the crew's teeth, shook loose anything not made fast, and sent the whole ship bucking and plunging like a frightened horse.

When the mortar was fired, that also lit a fuse in the bombshell itself. With luck, it exploded about the time it landed, scattering fragments far and wide. But not often. While every effort was made to cut the fuse to fit the distance, the shells were wildly erratic and quite likely to burst in midair.

At Baltimore, however, arithmetic was on Admiral Cochrane's side. A well-handled bomb vessel could hurl forty-five to fifty shells an hour, and he had five of them. With all that firepower—and safe from the annoyance of any return fire—the fall of Fort McHenry seemed only a matter of time.

Major George Armistead tried to coax just a little more range out of his guns. He had already increased the elevation as much as he could, but that wasn't enough. Now he loaded them with extra charges of powder—a dangerous experiment, since the barrels could only stand so much. Happily, they didn't burst, but three of the guns gave a mighty kick that threw them off their carriages. That could be fixed; the big problem remained. Armistead had tried everything, and the guns of Fort McHenry still couldn't reach the British fleet.

The best the fort could do was 1,800 yards with the twenty-four-pounders and 2,800 yards with the big French thirty-six-pounders. But since the British ships were over two miles out, he was just wasting his shots. At 10 A.M. Armistead grimly ordered his guns to cease fire, and the garrison settled down to a long, hard wait.

The gunners crouched by their parapets; the infantry huddled in a dry moat that ran around part of the fort. Trying to make himself small, Judge Nicholson felt that he and his Artillery Fencibles were all "like pigeons tied by the legs to be shot at."

By 9:30 A.M. Admiral Cochrane was feeling discouraged, too. He was meant to be helping the army, yet this flashy bombardment had been going on for two hours, and nothing had been accomplished. The firing was too slow; the shells were too erratic; and above all, the fort was too strong. He now dashed off a pessimistic note to Admiral Cockburn, presumably attacking by land with the troops:

My Dear Admiral—It is impossible for the ships to render you any assistance—the town is so far retired within the forts. It is for Colonel Brooke to consider under such circumstances whether he has force sufficient to defeat so large a number as it is said the enemy has collected, say 20,000 strong, or even a less number and to take the town. Without this can be done, it will be only throwing the men's lives away and prevent us from going upon other services. At any rate a very considerable loss must ensue and as the enemy is daily gaining strength, his loss let it be ever so great cannot be equally felt. . . .

Thus by midmorning caution was again creeping over Admiral Cochrane. He had given up all idea of supporting Colonel Brooke. He wasn't even sure the army should go through with its attack. But assuming the troops did take the city, the navy must continue battering at the fort, hoping ultimately to open a passage through which he could join Brooke, share the glory, and remove the riches of Baltimore. The five bombs pounded on—eleven . . . noon . . . 1 P.M. . . .

It was just about 2 P.M. when a British shell landed square on the southwest bastion of Fort McHenry and exploded with a blinding flash. For a brief second everything was lost in a ball of fire and smoke; then it cleared away, revealing a twenty-four-pounder dismounted and its crew sprawled at odd angles in the dirt.

Several members of Judge Nicholson's Fencibles rushed over —it was one of their guns—but they were too late to help Lieutenant Levi Claggett or Sergeant John Clemm, two of Baltimore's prominent merchants who served in the company. As the dead and wounded were carried off Private Philip Cohen must have felt lucky indeed. He had been standing right next to Claggett when the shell landed, yet he escaped without a scratch.

So many of the garrison seemed to live charmed lives. Captain Henry Thompson dashed through a hail of shrapnel, carrying messages to and from Hampstead Hill. As Commodore Rodgers' courier, Master's Mate Robert Stockton was constantly exposed. And every man in the garrison must have had a horseshoe in his pocket in that terrifying moment when a shell finally did crash through the roof of the magazine. It didn't go off, just lay there sputtering as some quick-witted hero doused the fuse in time.

This was too close a call for Major Armistead. He ordered the powder barrels cleared out and scattered under the rear walls of the fort. Better risk one or two than see the whole place go up.

Actually there was nothing else to do but trust in luck, and perhaps that was why the men took it as such a good omen when a rooster appeared from nowhere, mounted a parapet, and began to crow. The exhausted troops laughed and cheered, and one man called out that if he lived to see Baltimore again, he'd treat that bird to a pound cake.

Toward 3 P.M. Major Armistead suddenly noticed that three of the British bomb vessels had weighed anchor and, together with the rocket ship, were moving toward the fort again. Apparently Admiral Cochrane felt he had softened it up enough— that it could no longer hurt his ships even if they came within range. Now they were closing in for the kill.

That was all right with Armistead. For six hours he had sat taking his punishment, firing only occasionally to reassure Baltimore he was still holding out. But most of his guns were sound and his gunners thirsting for a chance to work off their frustrations. Now they stood at the embrasures, aching to go. The British ships glided closer—two miles, a mile and a half. Then with a roar that shook the whole harbor, Armistead let go with everything he had.

The *Devastation* shuddered as a cannonball plowed into her port bow, springing timbers and starting a leak. Another ripped through her main topsail. The *Volcano* took five straight hits—miraculously, none serious. A gunboat, observing fire three hundred yards ahead, caught a freak shot that cut a Royal Colonial Marine in half.

Admiral Cochrane quickly reversed himself. The fort wasn't finished after all. In fact, despite all those bombshells, it seemed barely damaged. Signal flags fluttered from the *Surprize*, ordering the squadron to disengage and pull back again out of range.

By now the Admiral felt more frustrated than ever. This long-range shelling was getting him nowhere, but what else was there to do? His frigate captains had an answer to that: they wanted to run the *Hebrus*, *Severn*, and *Havannah* right alongside the fort and blow the place out of the water. No, said Cochrane, that might cost too many men.

He was, in truth, the prisoner of his own policies. There was little point in taking Baltimore unless he could lay his hands on the immense wealth of the city, yet there was no way to do that without taking Fort McHenry, and no way to do that without risking high losses—the sort that might ruin his plans for the South and the even greater wealth of New Orleans.

By the same reasoning, Cochrane was more and more convinced that Brooke's land attack was pointless, and when he got a letter from Brooke asking that a diversionary action be mounted that night on the Ferry Branch of the Patapsco—on the other side of Baltimore—he wrote back counselling against the whole scheme. Communications broke down at this point, and although Brooke decided to take the more experienced officer's advice and abandon the whole offensive, no message to this effect got back to Cochrane. The Admiral, unable to tell what was happening on land, decided therefore that he must stage the diversion as requested.

To lead the diversionary action Cochrane picked Captain Charles Napier of the frigate *Euryalus*, one of his most enterprising officers. Around midnight Napier was to take a picked force of seamen and marines in small boats, lead them quietly—with muffled oars—into the Ferry Branch, west of Fort McHenry. Continuing a mile or a mile and a half, they were then to anchor and wait. At 1 A.M. the bombs would open up again on

Fort McHenry, and when signalled by skyrockets, Napier was to start firing, too. To make as much uproar as possible, he would use guns and rockets and mix in blank cartridges. It was all-important to put on a good show: "An attack is to be made upon their lines directly at two o'clock."

At 9 P.M. the fire of the bomb vessels slackened, then ceased altogether. Cochrane's hope was that the Americans would take this as the end of the day's work. At ten the small boats of Napier's squadron, loaded with men, came alongside the *Surprize* for final instructions. Morale was sky-high, but to add that extra ounce of fortitude a half ration of rum was passed out to the men.

Midnight, and they were on their way—twenty boats altogether, carrying perhaps three hundred men. It was raining hard now—a pitch-black night—and with the guns of the fort and the fleet both silent, there was absolutely nothing to guide them. The last eleven boats lost the others in the darkness, missed the turn west into the Ferry Branch, and continued rowing straight for Baltimore harbor. A less weary set of defenders might have seen them and caught them square between the guns of Fort McHenry and the Lazaretto. As it was, the lost boats managed to turn around and splash back to safety. Leaderless and confused, they returned to the *Surprize*.

Reduced to nine boats and 128 men, Captain Napier led the remainder of his flotilla into the Ferry Branch, unaware of the fiasco behind him. Sticking close to the far shore—oars muffled as directed—he slipped safely past Fort McHenry. Now he was passing Fort Babcock and soon would be opposite Fort Covington—two outlying strong points on the Ferry Branch. Here he planned to drop his hook and wait.

At Fort Babcock, Sailing Master John A. Webster cocked a shrewd ear to the roar of the British bomb vessels as they opened up at 1 A.M. It struck him that they were firing harder than ever and that this might mean trouble for him. He changed the charges in all six of his guns, this time double-shotting them with eighteen-pound balls and grapeshot. Finally satisfied, he wrapped himself in a blanket and, despite the rain, lay down on the breastwork for a nap.

He was dreaming of home when he suddenly jerked awake. He could hear the unmistakable sound of oars and sweeps. Ordering the men to their posts, Webster peered into the night, noticed an occasional dim light moving up the Ferry Branch about two hundred yards offshore. He quickly checked the priming and personally trained each of the guns, then gave the signal to open fire by shooting his pistol in the air. Just before 2 A.M. the battery thundered into action.

Five hundred yards upstream at Fort Covington, Lieutenant H. L. Newcomb also saw the lights and opened fire, some claimed even sooner than Webster. Then Captain Napier—realizing there was no longer any point in hiding—opened up, too. Fort McHenry joined in, and the British ships were firing their hardest. The fuses of their great two-hundred-pound bombshells traced fiery arcs across the sky, while flights of Congreve and signal rockets gave a weirdly festive look to this deadly serious night.

At Fort Babcock, Sailing Master Webster hammered away at the silhouettes of the British boats and felt sure he was getting some hits. But it was hard work manhandling these big eighteen-pounders, and he dislocated his shoulder in the process. Need-

CONTINUED ON PAGE 91

Francis Scott Key, 1779–1843

O say can you see ~~through~~ by the dawn's early light,
What so proudly we hail'd at the twilight's last gleaming,
Whose broad stripes & bright stars through the perilous fight
O'er the ramparts we watch'd, were so gallantly streaming?
And the rocket's red glare, the bomb bursting in air,
Gave proof through the night that our flag was still there,
O say does that star spangled banner yet wave
O'er the land of the free & the home of the brave?

Francis Scott Key apparently wrote out his untitled poem, now our national anthem, several times; the version above, although not the original, is in his handwriting. Below, a group of patriotic ladies is shown at work in 1914 restoring Fort McHenry's battered flag. Sewing it to a linen backing, the ladies saved as much of the huge, decaying flag as possible, and the pared-down restitution, measuring 28 by 32 feet, now hangs in the Museum of Science and Technology at the Smithsonian Institution in Washington, D.C.

WHAT MADE MAURY RUN

In December, 1936, Oswald Garrison Villard, longtime liberal editor of The Nation, *wrote his friend Representative Maury Maverick (1895-1954), of San Antonio, Texas, that he wanted to inform the public of the congressional burdens caused by the New Deal's economic emphasis. He asked that Maverick's secretary send him a statistical breakdown of a week in the life of a congressman.*

Deeply devoted to his job, the brash and boisterous Maverick had already, in the first of the two terms he would serve, won a national reputation by ignoring the protocol of silence observed by freshmen in the House. He had no patience with hypocrisy or with official language that obfuscated issues, for which he coined the word gobbledygook. *He was intensely proud of his colonial heritage, of his grandfather who had signed the Texas Declaration of Independence; and he saw, as his historic mission, the safeguarding of individuals' rights and the nation's natural resources. This same grandfather, Samuel Maverick, according to a frequently repeated legend, added a word to the English language when, probably through an oversight of his slaves, he failed to brand a small herd of cattle in his possession. Thereafter, "maverick" was the common name for an unbranded animal, and in time the word stood for a politician independent of party control. Maury Maverick, both in Congress and in a term as mayor of San Antonio, from 1939 to 1941, lived up to the name.*

The secretary's report indicated that Congressman Maverick received 150 letters and forty callers daily, attended up to six weekly committee meetings, and was often at his desk late into the night. During adjournment, there was some surcease, though the office seekers increased and the phone never stopped ringing. But the secretary's simple listing of statistics didn't tell of the "pangs and pains" or the "emotional strain" the congressman endures, so Maverick took pen to paper and did the job himself. —Barbara S. Kraft

In the first place, no one ever talks to a Congressman unless they are either unemployed, angry, or in a state of defeat. The "successful" men have no time to talk to a Congressman, and you receive no visits from your friends, because your office is always packed and jammed with unfortunate people demanding immediate attention. You are constantly besieged to make speeches, and you are supposed to make facetious remarks and tell two or three jokes—generally jokes which are wholly outside of the realm of thought—and then to make a very grave speech, complimenting the group you address.

It is impossible for a Congressman to walk down the street, even with his wife and children, or with his best friends or associates. Leaving the Maverick Building and going to the St. Anthony Hotel, which is only two short blocks, I am frequently stopped as many as ten or twenty times. Each person starts out by saying: "Congressman. Can I see you just a minute?" or "You're the hardest man to find in town. I've been trying to get you for six weeks." Or similar approaches. In biting cold weather, and already late, it is necessary to listen to a long story which has no point, with a great mass of irrelevant data,—all of which could have been handled as a routine matter by my secretary in the first place.

Point: There is absolutely no time for the average Congressman to study, make research, and improve his mind. His secretarial staff is insufficient for the amount of work. With large numbers of people calling all the time, the telephone ringing incessantly, and work to be done, the physical part of the task, the simple administrative duties, simply weight the Congressman down. It is perfectly natural, therefore, for Congressmen to break under the impact and give up entirely using their own brains.

Second point: Democracy is likely to break down of its own weight. After great hullabaloo, accusations and counter-accusations, a man is elected to office. Then the people prevent him from doing his duty. Strangely enough, in reference to Congressmen, the people have no respect at all for each other. Attempting to talk to one constituent means nothing to another—he will break in and start talking about his own affairs. I know that this is not the plight of the lawyer, businessman, or average citizen who is "prominent"—because before I was in Congress people talked to me one at a time.

Historical psychological background (in deep confidence): In times past, the royalty had a touch of magic. There is no royalty now, and no one to settle a man's problems. If he is a Catholic, he can go to a priest for confession and, I understand, get some consolation. But if he wants a pension, is out of a job, has been fired, has been given a dishonorable discharge from the Army and wants to get back in, is going to lose his home because he hasn't paid anything on his HOLC loan since he made it some 12 to 16 months before, or wants a job for a "friend," or has anything the matter with him at all, the only person who will even speak to him, or whom he can speak to, is the degraded remnant of royalty— the Congressman. Hence, no Congressman can walk down the streets of his home town naturally. He cannot stop at a shop window, because he will be pinched, slapped on the back, or jerked away and asked questions and told views until he gives up in disgust, calls a taxicab, and hides his head so he can get home and get away from it all.

As for Washington, the situation is not quite as bad, but there come all day long cranks of all kinds who have a "plan" to solve the depression, or a fool-proof "pension system," and most of them are good people who have some hold on you and you have to speak to them. I have an additional burden, and this is true of all Congressmen who are unfortunate enough to have Revolutionary, 1812, Mexican War, and Civil War relatives. Thank God there are no Abolitionists in my family, or I would break under the strain. But there are plenty of others —I think I have you beat by several generations of them.

Then in Washington life, it has a feature which is disgusting. You are invited to a supper, and frequently an important one. It is supposed to start at seven, and it starts at eight. It's supposed to close at nine, but then everyone makes a speech, it is impossible to get away, and sometimes they last until eleven or twelve o'clock. You go home, having eaten too much, smoked too much, and listened to too much tiresome bull; you sleep too late; get to your office late. You can't get in on account of the people blocking the door waiting to see you, and you have a mass of correspondence which you probably don't answer in the morning and which is deferred until that night. You get behind further and further.

When any man makes a speech who has some self-respect, he has to make research. This is almost impossible, and so you send to the Library to get your books. You, of course, cannot read a speech, because Congressmen don't listen, anyway, which

necessitates an extreme familiarity with your subject if you talk without manuscript. The result is frequently slipshod speeches.

I hand you herewith a typical example of correspondence which I received this morning—one of my friends, whom I have known for twenty-five years, suggests that I lack sincerity because I disagree with him on the Supreme Court. I have written him a very sharp letter and have told him to mind his own business—but the customary thing for most Congressmen is to write a letter and say they appreciate the suggestion, and so on.

I can truthfully state the following, of every Congressman:

Republican, or Democrat, he works harder than any two businessmen.

He is above average, and I do not believe that there is a single Member of Congress who would accept a bribe in money in any sum.

He is generally a better representative than his constituents deserve.

His health is bad because of his constant application to work, and statistics show that Congressmen die of acute indigestion, heart trouble of various kinds, such as coronary thrombosis, also arterio-sclerosis, and diseases due to improper diet.

He really wants to learn, study and apply himself, but conditions of being a modern messenger boy simply make it impossible.

Very truly yours,

Maury Maverick, M.C.

U.P.I.

Barbara S. Kraft, a former staff member of Kiplinger Washington Editors, is a candidate for a doctorate in history at The American University in Washington, D.C.

Utopia by the Lake

A lake steamer discharges passengers at Chautauqua's New Pier Building, ca. 1920.

One summer evening in the mid-1960's there was a concert on the porch of an old hotel in western New York State. Gingerbread pillars towered three stories into the darkness above the conductor, and figures leaning from the windows were silhouetted against the yellow rooms behind them. Below the porch, where the lawn sloped away to a lakeshore, the audience strolled back and forth or sat on the grass beneath old-fashioned Japanese lanterns that had been strung between the trees. As though on cue, a round, bright-orange harvest moon rose over the lake, making a white path across the water to the other shore. The orchestra swung into "The Blue Danube."

This scene, which might just as well have happened at the turn of the century, followed one of the most remarkable annual celebrations of ancestral piety in the United States. The hotel was the Athenaeum on Chautauqua Lake, in the Appalachian highlands ten miles above Lake Erie. The place was Chautauqua Institution, which was celebrating its ninetieth anniversary as a summer music festival and a resort of high culture. Earlier that evening, in the huge old wooden-roofed Amphitheatre set into the hill above the

By JEFFREY SIMPSON

hotel, five thousand people had gathered. There the assembly leader, standing on a platform in the pit of the Amphitheatre, read from a book lying open on the ornate walnut podium in front of him, just as other leaders had done every year since 1915:

The time is coming, when to the old question, "Who are here tonight who were present in 1874?" there will be no response,—a hush, a sudden turning to see if no one is there and then a solemn silence as the leader on that evening announces: "Not one." What year will that be? It must be a long time hence; for there were children in that auditorium on the

first night in 1874, who were but six years old, and who in 1944 will be seventy-six, and one or more of them may be present that season.

Then he asked the question; and a very old man in the front row rose feebly and tipped his hat.

The crowd burst into wild applause; they were honoring, really, what Chautauqua had meant during the old man's long life; in ninety years seven Presidents of the United States, opera singers, band leaders, revivalists, ambassadors, and aviators had come to Chautauqua. F.D.R. made his "I Hate War" speech here; Admiral Byrd, fresh

from the South Pole, had landed his plane on the golf course; and Teddy Roosevelt, who dropped by in 1904, called it "the most American place in America." And through it all, the earnestness, the sentimentality, and the idyllic atmosphere had prevailed.

Two dazzlingly successful gentlemen from the Midwest devised the notion of the first Chautauqua Assembly. The Reverend Dr. John Heyl Vincent, a Methodist minister from Galena, Illinois, met Lewis Miller, an Akron mill owner, inventor, and philanthropist, in the early 1870's. Miller had made a fortune from an invention called the Buckeye Mower, a reaper with the cutting arm hinged so that it could fit through a barn door. A devout churchgoer, Miller was looking around for new things to perfect and seized on the important ("as the twig is bent . . .") Sunday-school movement. Together the two men devised a summer training program for Sunday-school teachers. Miller, who provided the financial backing, suggested that a country location be found so that the benefits and attractions of a vacation could be added to the program.

They found the ideal site in Fair Point, a piece of land jutting out slightly into Chautauqua Lake in western New York, where the outdoor platform, tents, and log benches of a defunct camp meeting were for sale. Dr. Vincent, who was much later to become a bishop, had long hated camp-meeting hysteria and was trying to dissociate the Methodist Church from the phenomenon; he was particularly pleased to convert an old, dead meeting into the Chautauqua Lake Sunday School Assembly.

Letters were sent out, and 142 Sunday-school teachers came from twenty-five states, Canada, Ireland, Scotland, and India—from every corner of the Methodist world and its mission fields—to attend classes, which were held in four tents set in the grove of trees by the lakeshore. On that first evening, August 4, 1874, the two-week program of lectures and sermons opened with the singing of "Nearer, My God, to Thee" and various Scripture readings, beginning with "the day goeth away . . ." (Jeremiah 6:4), as in the light of pine-knot torches flaring in boxes of dirt an incredible two thousand local people sat jammed on log benches, swatting at mosquitoes coming up from the lake in the August dusk. (For ninety-eight years since, "Old First Night" has always begun with the same hymn and the same readings.) By August 12 an estimated ten to fifteen thousand people had flocked, walked, and sailed to the grounds to hear a particularly popular preacher, T. Dewitt Talmadge. It rained a lot those first seventeen days, but people just put up their umbrellas and stayed on, wading through the muck after each lecture to dripping tents, where they lodged and ate, or creaking away in wagons to the little towns around.

With the assembly burgeoning beyond their wildest expectations, Miller and Dr. Vincent decided to settle their families at Chautauqua the next summer. They built rustic cottages, half chalet and—because they were loath to lose the spontaneous camping atmosphere of the first season—half tent. Miller's cottage may have been the first prefab house to be assembled in America; painted white with raspberry trim, it had a white- and raspberry-striped canvas extension pitched on the verandah for guest bedrooms. The program was lengthened another week, to twenty-four days, and enrollment was opened to include members of any Christian denomination. Dr.

Vincent taught, among other subjects, classes on life in Biblical times and the geography of the Bible. A relief map of the Holy Land was constructed along the lakeshore, with tiny hills, white plaster villages, and a stagnant little Dead Sea; Chautauqua Lake served as the Mediterranean.

The curriculum was expanded, too, to include "night concerts on the lake," though it's not clear whether the musicians or the audience, or both, floated. In the afternoons, that second summer, there were "scientific *conversazioni*," and one lecturer donned the garb of a Middle Eastern shepherd to deliver a talk on "Jordan and Its People." A ramshackle, makeshift guest house, two stories of wooden framework with canvas walls inside, rose on the hill above the gingerbread cottages rapidly being thrown up by the first Sunday-school teachers, who had invited their families and boarders. The building was christened "Knower's Ark" because of the clever speakers who stayed there, and advertisements for the boarding houses (Sunday dinner with chicken: seventy-five cents) appeared in the new paper, *The Chautauqua Daily Assembly Herald*, along with schedules of lectures and musical events. The cottages, festooned with trimming as delicate as lacework, lost their rawness among the trees covering the grounds. And President Ulysses S. Grant, once a parishioner of Dr. Vincent's in Galena, sailed down Chautauqua Lake in a floating palace steamboat and set his seal of approval on the venture. God, education, the President, and the good life had met on the lakeshore. Chautauqua was a boom resort.

During Chautauqua's first summers the complexion of America was changing. Following the upheaval of the Civil War, the stable rural order of the early Republic was giving way to an urban and industrial society. A hundred sentimental paintings, the most famous Hovenden's *Breaking*

The cultural tone at Chautauqua was set by the cofounders—Methodist minister Dr. John Heyl Vincent (opposite) and business-man-inventor Lewis Miller (below). Miller's predilection for chalet architecture combined with tentlike porch extensions for guest bedrooms was widely copied. Dr. Vincent started the Chautauqua Literary and Scientific Circle, a do-it-yourself educational course. Each year there was a graduation ceremony that included a procession like the one at right, photographed in 1904, including Dr. Vincent and theologian Jesse L. Hurlbut bringing up the rear. Mrs. Vincent is the formidable lady in the dark dress. The young girl is Margaret McGrew Copeland, who later was the community's archivist for many years, up to the time of her death in 1971. She helped select the photographs accompanying this story.

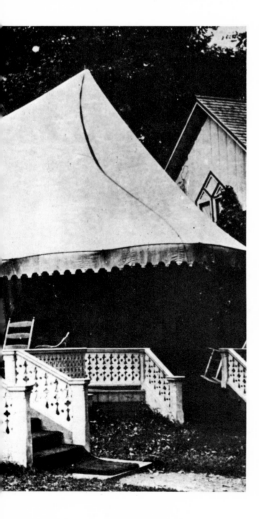

Home Ties, depicted country boys leaving farms for the lure of the city and regular wages. This movement had created a big market for nostalgia; if you hadn't made it in the city, the grinding routine of the farm seemed awfully secure, and even if you had made it, the old home town took on the hazy outlines of a much-loved memory. Chautauqua, born of a much older American yearning—the hunger for education—bloomed in this climate as an ideal country village where people beginning to cherish the memory of a departed agrarian society could spend several bucolic, informative weeks every summer.

By the third summer, in 1876, Chautauqua was established beyond a doubt. The program now ran eight weeks, from the first Sunday in July to the last Sunday in August, and Frances E. Willard, founder of the Women's Christian Temperance Union, became the first woman speaker to appear on the lecture stage, thrilling everyone with stories about the horrors of drink. This was the hundredth year of the Republic, and the Philadelphia Centennial Exposition was supposed to draw all the crowds who had the money and leisure to travel. But so potent was Chautauqua's appeal that three assemblies—one in Michigan, one on an island in the St. Lawrence River, and one in Iowa—were set up in imitation of the original, complete with tents, boarding houses, silver-tongued orators, and lectures on the Holy Land.

Two years later a permanent roofed, open-air Amphitheatre was built into the hillside, and the Grecian Hall of Philosophy (also called "the Hall in the Grove") rose. Within a few years two-decker steamboats were landing at the three-decker pier building with its ice-cream pagodas, a tower, and a flag. And by 1881 the Hotel Athenaeum, modelled after the Grand Union at Saratoga, had replaced the old canvas Palace Hotel. The Athenaeum had gingerbread

pillars three stories high on the sweeping verandahs and a cupola so top-heavy that it had to be torn down in the 1920's because its weight was pushing the rooms below through the foundations. The story goes that there was no loom in the United States big enough to weave carpets for the acres of polished Athenaeum floor, so the builders had to send to France. The Athenaeum's parlors had, of course, no place for dancing or card playing, and the dining room was completely "dry." The diversions at Chautauqua were for the mind.

For people who couldn't get to Chautauqua, Dr. Vincent started in 1878 the Chautauqua Literary and Scientific Circle—the first book club and correspondence course in America. This was a four-year course: the first one offered the chief civilizations of the world; later there were courses on history, literature, and science. The response was overwhelming. All over the land, farmers, storekeepers, and their wives met in village groups one afternoon a month to talk about things that once only a preacher might have known. A group in an Iowa town debated what Aristotle's teachings meant, while in Ohio another pondered Napoleon's campaigns. A letter from a farmwife explaining to the circle's secretary why she was late with her assignment expresses the terrible hunger

Life at Chautauqua early became a curious mixture of inspirational lectures and summer pleasures. At top right is the busy plaza outside the post office after a morning lecture in 1915. The sedate couple seated outside the Victorian cottage (top left) are Jacob Miller, brother of the co-founder, and wife, about 1878. Next below is the community's baseball team, obviously all college athletes, around 1898. At right is one of the many boarding houses, this one catering to the culture-hungry of Beaver County, Pennsylvania, about 1888. The hotel at far right, still in use, is the venerable Athenaeum, at the turn of the century.

Ever since Ulysses S. Grant's visit to Chautauqua in 1875, a year after it was founded, celebrities have been attracted to the community's idyllic setting. The touching scene above greeted Teddy Roosevelt in 1904. Wire hoops help the uppermost little girls keep their poise.

Left: Nosegays were in abundance one summer day in 1929 when the Women's Club feted Mrs. Henry Ford (seated, wearing hat) and Mrs. Thomas Edison (at her right). Below, left and right: Dr. Vincent with an uneasy Chinese diplomat, about 1904; and with feminist leader Jane Addams, 1915. Above: Amelia Earhart poses with the Bestor family, 1929.

that Chautauqua somehow filled:

I live on a farm, and my husband has no help except what I give him. All of the time I am not doing housework, I am obliged to drive the horse at the horse-power . . . I have done my reading while driving the horse for the last two months, but I cannot write while driving.

Each year, when a four-year course was completed, there was a graduation ceremony, known as Recognition Day, at Chautauqua for all the readers who could get there. The old Grecian Hall of Philosophy was replaced in the early 1900's by a temple modelled on the Parthenon. A long walkway led up to this new Hall of Philosophy from a white archway at the foot of the walk. On Recognition Day a gilded wooden gate was hung in the arch, and the graduates literally went through the Golden Gate, led—as a photograph from 1910 shows—by sixty flower girls, in pairs, who strewed the path with gladiolas, daisies, and roses as the graduates passed under the arch. The diplomas carried arcane terms conferring distinction, depending upon how many books a graduate had read. There was a seal for each reading course completed, a special seal (which nearly everyone got) for having read through the Bible, and, highest of all, for the reader of numerous books beyond the assigned number, membership in the "Guild of the Seven Seals." But these honors, faintly smelling of the fraternal lodge, were not really what Recognition Day was about. As Dr. Vincent wrote, the Chautauqua Literary and Scientific Circle was meant for

ambitious people who still foster "ideals," who in good health although no longer young, hope and resolve to go on and on and up and "higher yet" until they shall be accounted among those "who are worthy to be crowned."

And Recognition Day was

when the "Golden Gate" shall be opened and children with their baskets of flowers,

conforming to customs from time immemorial, will strew with blossoms the pathway of pilgrims under the arches of the "Hall on the Hill."

In other words, study was a way to salvation, and graduating was heaven. Which was probably not an exaggerated metaphor for the whole new world that circle books offered the lady who had to help her husband "at the horsepower."

As part of the same impulse to provide culture and refinement to the world, the leaders of Chautauqua chartered Chautauqua University, and for a while an accredited degree was given. The charter was dropped in 1890, when the leaders realized that Chautauqua was never meant to give academic credit. The preachers and doctors and schoolteachers who came already had degrees, and everybody else who came had worked for a lifetime without one. They wanted Chautauqua's "culture and refinement" because they were starved for it, not because it carried a degree. Besides, there was more prestige in studying because you didn't have to than in studying because you did. Chautauqua offered culture as a status symbol and as a vaguely transcendental means of salvation to an America that was ready for it on both counts. President James A. Garfield, the third President to visit, after Grant and Rutherford P. Hayes, said that Chautauqua was trying to "open out fields of thought, to open out ener-

Chautauqua was strong on pageantry, falling back on an apparently inexhaustible supply of nubile maidens, like the angels shown at right above. What they are heralding has long since been forgotten. Below is a detachment of junior angels, strewing the path with flowers during the annual grand parade of the Chautauqua Literary and Scientific Circle; it is Recognition Day, 1918. Everyone is suitably serious, for the graduates are approaching the archway to the Hall of Philosophy.

gies, a largeness of mind, a culture in the better senses, with the varnish scratched off."

There were dissident voices, however, even then. One of the clearest, cutting through the summer air, belonged to William James, the psychologist and brother of the novelist. Raised in the East and in Europe and steeped in much older, rooted cultures, James was appalled by the brushed-on stuff at Chautauqua. He admitted that he had been temporarily pleased by the facilities and amenities:

I went in curiosity for a day. I stayed for a week, held spellbound by the charm and ease of everything, by the middle-class paradise, without a sin, without a victim, without a blot, without a tear.

And yet . . .

And yet what was my own astonishment, on emerging into the dark and wicked world again, to catch myself quite unexpectedly and involuntarily saying: "Ouf! what a relief! Now for something primordial and savage, even though it were as bad as an Armenian massacre, to set the balance straight again. This order is too tame, this culture too second-rate, this goodness too uninspiring. This human drama without a villain or a pang; this community so refined that ice-cream soda-water is the utmost offering it can make to the brute animal in man; this city simmering in the tepid lakeside sun; this atrocious harmlessness of all things, I cannot abide with them . . . in this unspeakable Chautauqua there was no potentiality of death in sight anywhere, and no point of the compass visible from which danger might possibly appear. . . ."

Bourgeoisie and mediocrity, church sociables and teachers' conventions, are taking the place of the old heights and depths and romantic chiaroscuro. And,

to get human life in its wild intensity, we must in future turn more and more away from the actual, and forget it, if we can, in the romancer's or the poet's pages. The whole world, delightful and sinful as it may still appear to one just escaped from the Chautauquan enclosure, is nevertheless obeying more and more just those ideals that are sure to make of it in the end a mere Chautauqua Assembly on an enormous scale. . . . Even now, in our own country, correctness, fairness, and compromise for every small advantage are crowding out all other qualities. The higher heroisms and the old rare flavors are passing out of life.

Most people, however, thought Chautauqua was doing extraordinarily good work. By 1886 more than thirty imitation assemblies had sprung up, most of them faithful copies and most of them with Dr. Vincent's blessing. Sometime in the 1890's travelling tent shows, unauthorized by the parent Chautauqua, picked up the commercially hot Chautauqua name and offered a combination of popular music and political oratory all over the Midwest. The travelling Chautauquas watered down their culture; as a result, Booker T. Washington or Billy Sunday would find a trained seal or Swiss bell-ringers on the same program with him. William Jennings Bryan's favorite platform was a travelling Chautauqua tent, and he said in 1914:

The privilege and opportunity of addressing from one to seven thousand of his fellow Americans, in the Chautauqua frame of mind, in the mood which almost as clearly asserts itself under the tent or amphitheatre as does reverence under the "dim religious light"—this privilege and this opportunity is one of the greatest that any patriotic American could ask.

The travelling Chautauquas, like the original, became national organs of communication. Anything said at Chautauqua was sure to be heard—all over the Midwest, at least. When, in 1904, Teddy Roosevelt called Chautauqua "the most American place in America," he really was

acknowledging the same quality that appealed to Bryan and repelled William James: the American dream of the educated pastoral man, the utopia in the wilderness.

And everybody came to Chautauqua. The Studebakers built a "cottage" at Chautauqua, as did a cadet branch of the Heinz family. The Brown shoe people from St. Louis came for the season, and so did the Norths, who owned the Ringling Brothers and Barnum & Bailey Circus. The queen of the summer people, at the very top of Chautauqua's society, was Lewis Miller's daughter, Mina, who had married Thomas Edison in 1886. Cars and pickles and Buster Brown shoes and circuses and the electric light bulb—the staples of home life were the support of Chautauqua, the ideal village.

Although the program got more and more sophisticated, with symphony concerts and Russian choirs, and although a yacht club was formed and an athletic program started by Alonzo Stagg flourished, nevertheless life was as strictly regulated as ever. There was a service each day in the Amphitheatre at 9:30 A.M., directed by the chaplain of the week, who had preached to a capacity crowd of eight thousand the preceding Sunday; at eleven some political or literary lecturer spoke; and in the evening there was another lecture or concert in the Amphitheatre. The afternoon was reserved for games and naps and club meetings. Bats—so the story goes—had been imported and encouraged to eat the mosquitoes, but otherwise there wasn't much more comfort than in the first days. The hotels and boarding houses, from the grand Athenaeum dominating the lakefront to flimsy structures with crazy stacked porches leaning against the side of a ravine, housed people either wild for culture or compelled to seem so. It was surely the least relaxing resort ever conceived. The hotel help, usually college students or schoolteachers, couldn't clear the tables fast enough lest they miss some "event"; Alexander Woollcott, when he was a Hamilton College undergraduate in 1907, wrote from Chautauqua to a friend:

You needn't sniff at my occupation for the summer. Almost all the waiters at Chautauqua are college men and we get our board and room for our pains. All we have to do is to come at meal times, serve our table and clear it away. . . . It's a great place with six or eight entertainments every day all free. They have the finest music . . . of any resort in the country. . . . Last week they had the Prize Spelling Match. . . . I went in for New Jersey and covered her with glory by missing the first word they gave me.

The grounds, lying along the lakeshore for about a mile and a half and stretching a half mile up the hill, were encircled, except along the lakeshore, by an iron fence of palings six feet high. There was a gate at the boat dock where the steamers arrived and a wicket gate at the top of the hill, which for a while in the early 1900's was connected by interurban streetcars to the railroad station three miles away. For years after they appeared, no automobiles were allowed in—and to this day they're only permitted to load and unload baggage. The sole vehicles on the grounds in those days were huge baggage wagons, which loaded up at the boat dock with Saratoga trunks and then wound along shady lanes between wedding-cake tiers of porches, distributing their cargo until they got to the road gate, where they picked up another load and worked their way back down to the dock. Eventually, when contributions no longer supported Chautauqua—after the Depression—the fence came in handy; then people were charged a single admission fee to the grounds, the fee covering all the programs. But in the early 1900's

the fence still served its original purpose: to set Chautauqua apart and underline the discipline it took to get Christian culture. On Saturday night the gates were locked, and all through the Sabbath ten thousand people stayed locked in— until Monday morning only medical emergencies got through. Stories linger today of people impaled on the fence while smuggling in Sunday papers or tobacco.

Life on the grounds at Chautauqua loosened up ever so slightly after World War I; some college students were permitted to dance even the Charleston in 1930, and Chautauqua's resort aspect became a little more evident. For one thing, Chautauqua was outmoded as a national forum. The radio, the Ford, and the movies had completely killed the travelling Chautauquas in the twenties; people didn't need to wait in some snowbound village all year for a week of lectures. For similar reasons, the Amphitheatre also lost its place as a national podium.

But as the program was released from the necessity of being all things to all Americans, instruction no longer had to be the guiding aim. Arthur Bestor, a former history professor who was president of the institution and program chairman from 1915 until 1944, brought the first opera to Chautauqua in 1926—sung, typically, in English—and created the Chautauqua Symphony in 1929. That same year a very modern gray concrete-enclosed theatre was built, all angular planes and purple glass lanterns reminiscent of both Bauhaus and an eighteenth-century gazebo, for the Chautauqua Opera Company and the summer repertory company of the Cleveland Playhouse. A lady from Pittsburgh wrote home to her puzzled family that her party stood in line after the opera, in evening dress, to get ice-cream cones at the vine-covered pergola by the post office. The "utmost offering . . . to the brute animal in man" was

CHAUTAUQUA ECSTASY

Alexander Woollcott's remark about failing in the spelling match at Chautauqua brought back a vivid memory of my own brief sojourn at that gathering of uplift and culture. My father was a Congregational minister, and one summer in the early twenties our whole family spent a week at Chautauqua. Family spelling bees had long been one of our favorite diversions, and all of us were pretty good—but Father, of course, was perfect. He could spell anything, and we all knew it. So on the hot night of the big Chautauqua spelling match, it didn't take much urging to get him up on the platform and into the contest. Mother and my two sisters and I sat there proudly, already sure of the glory that soon would be ours when Father spelled down everybody. All went as anticipated—for a while. With a sonorous pulpit delivery that carried clearly across the crowded auditorium, Father unhesitatingly spelled out "desuetude," "desiccate," "queue," and "inoculate." Several competitors had gone down to defeat when the contest master turned to Father and said, *Ecstasy.* For just a fraction of a second it seemed to us that Father faltered. But only a fraction; then his familiar, confident voice rang out: "Ecstasy. E-C-S-T-A-C-Y." There was a moment of dead silence. "Wrong," said the judge. We gasped. The unthinkable had happened, as if George Washington had admitted telling a lie. Looking ineffably crestfallen, Father descended and came slowly up the aisle. Later, back home, my grandmother made us all feel a *little* better. "Ecstasy!" she said—"Humph! It's not the kind of word a respectable person has any use for, anyway." —*E.M.H.*

still "ice-cream soda-water."

Looking at the pictures of the twenties and early thirties (the institution kept an official photographer), one is struck by the social nature of events—an echo, perhaps, of that false tranquillity that the world outside the Chautauqua fence felt between the wars. The ushers for the interdenominational Amphitheatre church service, young men from the best old Chautauqua families, stand in handsome rows like a chorus line, jutting chins topping Arrow collars, in blue blazers and white flannels. Genial Dr. Bestor, who grabbed every celebrity he could find for the capacity crowds in the Amphitheatre, had Amelia Earhart to tea with his family under an arbor, all of them looking stabbingly happy and young. At other times he was host to Governor Alfred E. Smith of New York, theologian Harry Emerson Fosdick, and composer George Gershwin, who wrote his Concerto in F in one of the practice sheds on the grounds.

In 1929, with the help of Mrs. Edison, Dr. Bestor staged "The Festival of Light," a joint celebration of the centenary of cofounder Lewis Miller's birth and the fiftieth anniversary of the invention of the electric light. It was ironic, really. Thomas Edison had never liked Chautauqua —he thought it was humbug—and while Mrs. Edison spent the season there, he was off on camping trips with his friends Henry Ford, Harvey Firestone, and Warren Harding. But Dr. Bestor and Mrs. Edison asked him, so he came, bringing Henry Ford and publisher Adolph Ochs with him. Mrs. Edison entertained Mrs. Ford on the white-pillared porch of the Women's Club, and the ladies had their pictures taken, seated in rocking chairs, holding nosegays. On an evening late in July, with eight thousand people in the Amphitheatre and another two thousand standing around the rim, Dr. Bestor, Edison, Ford, and Ochs stood on the platform with the Chautauqua Sym-

phony Orchestra behind them. "The Star-Spangled Banner" was played, the flag waved overhead, and the light shed by electricity, by Chautauqua, and by America on all the world was celebrated.

That was the climax in a way, though Chautauqua endures. It went bankrupt during the Depression, and all the old trees covering the grounds were sold—not to be cut down but to have little tin strips fastened on them with the names of donors to the Chautauqua Foundation.

The program continues today. There are still the symphony, operas, plays, and the summer school. The special events of the past few seasons have included a typical eclectic jumble of Van Cliburn, the Mormon

Tabernacle Choir, and Peter Nero. Robert F. Kennedy spoke there the summer before his death, and Marian Anderson gave one of her last concerts in the Amphitheatre.

There are still few cars and, supposedly, no liquor. The tranquil summer air is heavy with the scent of hollyhocks, and the sound of tennis balls makes a counterpoint to the orchestra rehearsal in the distance. But somewhere the utopian ideal froze, and Chautauqua became less a place of pilgrimage and emulation and more, perhaps, a memory of childhood—and an irrecoverable dream.

Jeffrey Simpson, a member of the staff of Horizon *magazine, has spent all twenty-six summers of his life at Chautauqua.*

A familiar scene at summer's end, this one from about 1905: trunks are lined up on the wharf of the Old Pier Building, awaiting the arrival of the lake steamer. The woman on the porch seems especially sad; is that only a cinder she is wiping from her eye?

A Cycle of Cathay

CONTINUED FROM PAGE 8

law wherever they went; their diplomatic protectors were allowed to reside in Peking at last; and their merchants and missionaries were permitted unrestricted access to the Chinese hinterland.

Although Americans had played the role of bystanders in the days of the Opium War, their cousinly instincts got the better of them in the later years of the century. In June, 1859, for instance, Commodore Josiah Tattnall, USN, instructed merely to observe while the British and French taught the recalcitrant Chinese a lesson off the approaches to Tientsin, grew alarmed at the successful Chinese resistance, went to the relief of the wounded British admiral, and ordered his men to help man the British guns. "Blood," he announced, in a sentence that has outlived his name, "is thicker than water." Forty-one years later the Commodore's instincts of consanguinity were confirmed by the participation of several thousand American troops in the German-led international expedition to put down the Boxer Rebellion and punish the Chinese government. And thereafter, for decades, American Army and Marine units were to be routinely stationed on Chinese soil, at Peking and Tientsin, while American gunboats patrolled the Yangtze River.

Large American fortunes had been built on the China trade before and after the Opium War, and the new treaty-port system promised even greater rewards. Indeed, the 1850's—the days of the clipper ships—were a brief moment when American tonnage in the China trade actually exceeded that of Great Britain. This was also a decade in which American vessels participated heavily in a trade even more reprehensible than the shipment of opium: the traffic in Chinese coolie laborers, abducted or otherwise procured in the South China region and shipped for hard labor and, more often than not, early death in Latin America. To recall only one appalling event in this grim chapter: there is the case of the *Waverley*, an American ship with a human cargo en route from China to South America, in whose hold 260 Chinese died of suffocation in September, 1855. Meanwhile, opium itself was being shipped by fast American steamers into Formosa as late as 1872—there to be smuggled into mainland coastal markets.

The 1850's were a special case, a peak in the trade relationship. Thereafter America's Civil War and postwar industrialization turned that nation inward for a while. Yet the new lure of the allegedly limitless China market would fascinate American entrepreneurs from the 1880's onward. And when that still mythical market seemed about to be closed off in 1899–1900 because of new European incursions into China, Washington pressed

for the famous open-door policy so that Americans would not be completely frozen out.

Meanwhile, before and after, American adventurers risked their fortunes in the newly evolving multinational cultures of the treaty ports—most notably Shanghai, near the mouth of the Yangtze River. A modest Chinese town prior to the Opium War, Shanghai had grown by the turn of the century into China's greatest seaport. Dwarfing the old Chinese city was a French concession of spacious tree-lined boulevards (after World War I the street names would be Avenue Pétain, Avenue Joffre, Avenue Foch). There was also a Japanese concession across Soochow Creek and a thriving International Concession under British domination, with a famous riverfront (called the Bund), parks, Sikh policemen, a racecourse, hotels, department stores, and teeming night life. Shanghai and lesser treaty ports were curious Sino-Western enclaves, utterly alien from traditional and village China.

As it turned out, the fabled China market was never to materialize. American trade with Japan always exceeded the China trade in the twentieth century. But the vision of four hundred million (or five hundred, or six hundred million) customers never lost its hold.

The greatest beneficiary, however, of the new and easier access to China after 1860 was not the merchant community but that other major segment of the American transpacific thrust, the Protestant mission movement.

American hopes for China's conversion to Christianity had their roots in early nineteenth-century revivalism in New England and New York State. Although individual missionaries, early arrivals at the Canton factories, played a significant role from time to time as interpreters of China back home and as aides to U.S. diplomats abroad, their impact on China remained infinitesimal in terms of converts. By the late 1800's and the first three decades of the twentieth century, however, the mission movement had proliferated into a multiple effort to transform Chinese society through education, medicine, and technology as well as the more traditional route of evangelism, all in the course of trying to "win China for Christ."

In the waning years of the dynasty—back in the "Age of Contempt"—American churchmen had often found the Chinese to be obdurate, vicious, and degenerate as well as simply unreceptive. As even a fairly enlightened mission leader and historian, S. Wells Williams, had written in 1858, "We shall get nothing important out of the Chinese unless we stand in a menacing attitude before them. They would grant nothing unless fear stimulated their sense of justice, for they are among the most craven of people, cruel and selfish as heathenism can make men, so we must be backed by force if we wish them to listen to reason."

But after 1905, and especially after the revolution of 1911, the missionaries were filled with warm sympathies and high hopes for their Chinese protégés, freed at last from the bonds of Confucianism and ready, it seemed, for Christianity as well as democracy. Such sympathies and hopes were shared, it should be added, by a succession of American statesmen in Washington, from William Howard Taft and Woodrow Wilson right on into the 1940's. It is ironic that these optimistic predictions flourished against a background of decades of legislation that systematically excluded Chinese from immigration and citizenship.

What is important to the Sino-American relationship is not merely the outlook of missionaries and their considerable impact as trainers, through their schools, colleges, and hospitals, of a new generation of Chinese. What is also important is the role they played—and they were some five thousand strong by the mid-1920's —as conveyors of images of China to their congregations and countrymen back home. Likewise significant were the views they helped to shape among large groups of Americans who came to believe in China as the most promising field abroad for American altruism and the export of would-be benevolence.

It is therefore hardly surprising that when, in the 1930's, a Chinese leadership emerged that was republican (at least in form), to some extent Christian (Chiang Kai-shek became a Methodist in 1931), and both anti-Communist and anti-Japanese, it would stimulate those deep-rooted hopes for the American role in China that both traders and missionaries had developed over more than a century of contact.

With the Japanese attack on Pearl Harbor in December, 1941, those hopes of private citizens and nonofficial groups were suddenly transformed into government policy—an open-ended alliance between Washington and the embattled Nationalist wing of the Chinese revolution. But that Nationalist wing, more a faction than a government, was already in deep trouble. And it was to fall victim, before long, to the renewed and invigorated assault of its old Communist rivals.

So trade and religion—gold and God—in all their complex ramifications seem to lie at the root of America's people-to-people relationship with China.

It need hardly be added that neither gold nor God did the trick. The Chinese, stirred very roughly out of their two-thousand-year-old world order, took off on a path very different from that prescribed by capitalism and Christianity. To fill the social, ethical, and political vacuum left by the collapse of Confucianism, they eventually created Maoism—a new civic religion. And in place of the unequal treaties and foreign tutelage they

James Thomson, a member of the East Asian Research Center at Harvard University, lectures on history there but is likely to be more familiar to readers as one of the experts who appeared on the ABC-TV network to furnish commentary during President Nixon's trip to China.

substituted national self-reliance and the expulsion of all foreign tutors—including, finally, the Russians. As for the impact of a century of trade and religion in Sino-American relations, the one was written off by the new regime as economic imperialism, the other as cultural imperialism.

After the Communist victory in 1949 American leaders misread China's revolutionary transformation and sought to seal off the apparent threat of a new Golden Horde, a new Yellow Peril. But by 1972 an American President had belatedly ended that effort. Ironically, but also appropriately, he had returned instead to the role of earnest visitor knocking at China's long-closed door, as foreigners had done two centuries before.

As one reflects on the roller coaster of fluctuating American attitudes toward China and the Chinese, one wonders how the new age that began with Ping-Pong and Kissinger will be described by historians of the future. If it is an "Age of Euphoria," it will be short-lived and its sequel unpleasant, for euphoria is flimsy stuff indeed for the bridging of the very wide gulf between Chinese and Americans. But if instead it develops into an "Age of Live, Let Live, and Learn," the Nixon chapter could help produce new qualities of realism and understanding among both Americans and Chinese that previous chapters have lacked.

"My English isn't so hot. As near as I can make out, it says 'Cronkite was here.'"

DRAWING BY LORENZ; © 1972 THE NEW YORKER MAGAZINE, INC.

ing more hands, he sent a young midshipman named Andrews to get back thirty men he had previously lent Lieutenant George Budd, a half mile to the rear.

Budd refused to release them. He needed every man, he explained, to cover Webster's retreat when the British drove him from the shore. This gloomy appraisal was too much for young Andrews. Instead of reporting back to Webster, he galloped off to Baltimore, spreading the news that Fort Babcock was lost.

Baltimore was almost ready to believe him. Every building in town shook from the explosions. The rain-swept sky flickered and flared with the flash of bursting bombshells. To the spectators who crowded the city's rooftops, it was hard to see how anyone could get through this "most awful spectacle." And it might be only the start. For there was also the British army to consider, lurking, they believed, in the silent blackness beyond Hampstead Hill.

It was about 3 A.M. when the orders went out in the British camp to get everyone up. Lieutenant George Laval Chesterton, Royal Artillery, tried to uncurl from his square yard of floor in a crowded barn. His friend Captain Mitchell of the Marines had an easier time—he was quartered all alone in a pigsty.

Several hundred yards to the north, three other captains were called in from the best billet of all—Surrey, the fine country place of Colonel Joseph Sterett, currently with his regiment on Hampstead Hill. As they left one of them paused long enough to leave a waggish thank-you note on the dining-room sideboard:

Captains Brown, Wilcox and McNamara of the 53rd Regiment, Royal Marines, have received everything they could desire at this house, notwithstanding it was received at the hands of the butler, and in the absence of the colonel.

Spirits were high as the men fell in. Off toward the harbor they could hear the guns of the naval bombardment; they could see the flashes and trails of fire. The fleet was doing its part; soon it would be their turn. They were greatly outnumbered—one look at the American campfires on Hampstead Hill told them that—but they had handled militia before; they would do it again tonight.

Shortly after three the columns began moving—but not toward Hampstead Hill. To the general (but perhaps not universal) dismay of the troops, they were heading in the opposite direction. Away from the hill, away from Baltimore, away from the sound of the fight. As decided at the midnight council of war, Colonel Brooke was returning to North Point and the ships. The British forces were retreating, as one officer put it bitterly, "before a parcel of fellows who had scarcely even seen a gun fired in their lives . . . a parcel of tailors and shoemakers."

In the Ferry Branch, Captain Napier was beginning to wonder. Admiral Cochrane's orders said to keep firing until he saw the army was "seriously engaged," then return to the *Surprize*. But it was now after 3 A.M. and still no gun flashes—no rumble of cannon—from the hills to the east.

Something must have gone wrong. In any case, he had done his part: surely by now he had diverted all the Americans who could be diverted. So far he had miraculously escaped getting hit, but to stay any longer was courting disaster for no conceivable purpose. Signal lights flickered; Napier's boats swung around and began the long row home.

Passing Fort McHenry, they again hugged the far shore and almost slipped by unnoticed. But one of the officers chose this moment to fire a signal rocket to let the fleet know they were returning. The fort instantly responded with a hail of balls and grapeshot. Later, the British claimed only one boat was "slightly struck" and one man mortally wounded; the Americans, however, found the remains of at least two boats and the bodies of three seamen.

At 4 A.M. the boats were again alongside the *Surprize*, and the bombardment came to an end. Two or three of the vessels continued to take an occasional shot, but to all intents the fireworks were over, and the whole blazing, tumultuous night gave way to predawn quiet.

Francis Scott Key wondered what this sudden quiet meant as he stood with John S. Skinner and old Dr. Beanes on the deck of their flag-of-truce sloop. They were anchored with the transports some eight miles down the Patapsco—well out of the fight, yet near enough to follow most of the action. All day they had watched Fort McHenry's flag with a glass and knew it was still holding out. During the night the bombs and rockets were proof in themselves that Armistead had not surrendered. But this eerie, unexpected silence, broken only by an occasional distant gun, gave no hint to the fate of the fort—or the city itself.

Key found himself torn with anxiety. It was the climax of the whole soul-searing experience he had been going through these past days. He loathed "this abominable war," yet here he was in the middle of it. He saw himself as a gentleman who could be quite at ease with the polished English officers, but he found them to be, with few exceptions, "illiberal, ignorant and vulgar . . . filled with a spirit of malignity against everything American." He detested the saber-rattling rowdiness of Baltimore—sometimes felt the place deserved any punishment it got—but now it was fighting for its life, and he knew where his heart really lay. He was first and last an American, and in these hours of suspense he fervently—desperately—prayed that the flag was still there.

The three Americans paced the deck, scarcely daring to think what daylight might bring. Again and again they pulled out their watches, trying to gauge when the dawn would come. Five o'clock, and the first light of day at last tinged the sky. Out came the spyglass, but it was still too dark to make anything out. At 5:50 it was officially sunrise, but there was no sun today. The rain clouds hung low, and patches of mist swirled across the water, still keeping the night's secret intact.

But it was growing brighter all the time, and soon an easterly breeze sprang up, flecking the Patapsco and clearing the air. Once again Key raised his glass—and this time he saw it. Standing out against the dull gray of the clouds and hills was Major Armistead's American flag.*

Capping the joy of the three Americans, at 7 A.M. the *Surprize* signalled the bombarding squadron to retire down the river, at eight the *Erebus* and the five bombs were under way, and at nine the supporting frigates followed. The attack on Fort McHenry was over.

The turbulent, fervent thoughts racing through Francis Scott Key's mind began to take poetic shape. Using the back of a letter that happened to be in his pocket, he began to jot down lines and phrases and likely couplets . . .

Even on the fifteenth, when the enemy army was clearly re-embarking, Sam Smith remained cautious. He felt the move might be just preliminary to hitting Baltimore from another angle. That evening General Douglass' brigade prepared to thwart an assault on the south side of the city, and Sam Smith warned Fort McHenry that he believed "an attack would be made in the course of the night on this post and on the city by way of the Ferry Branch."

It was a bad moment for Fort McHenry to face such a prospect. Exhausted by five days of superhuman effort, Major Armistead was delirious with fever, and his subordinates were fighting over seniority. A new British attack would catch the place torn with dissension. Sam Smith hurriedly put Commodore Rodgers in charge. A little unorthodox, perhaps, to have a naval officer run an army fort, but as with most of Sam Smith's solutions, it worked.

On September 16 Cochrane's ships still hovered off North Point, but they were anchored out in the Bay now. Slowly, imperceptibly, it finally dawned on Baltimore's defenders that they had actually accomplished what they scarcely dared hope —they had turned back the British. At Fort McHenry the men

found it hard to believe that only three days ago they were crouching behind the ramparts, praying for their lives and relying on such a dubious talisman as a rooster crowing on the rampart. But one man remembered—and bought the rooster the pound cake he had promised.

On Hampstead Hill the troops were released from the earthworks and marched back to their regular quarters. Free from tension at last, the men exploded with a ribald joy that appalled Private John A. Dagg, a sometime clergyman from Virginia: "During the last few days every one had spoken softly and seriously, and no oaths had been heard, but this night our barracks were in an uproar with noise and profanity, giving painful proof of human depravity."

The noise and foolishness soon gave way to a deeper, quieter gratitude. For Baltimore it had been a very near thing, and everyone sensed it. Gifts poured in for the comfort of the wounded—not just money and medical supplies, but small things, too, from people who had little else to give except their thanks: two large pots of preserves from Mrs. Samuel Harris, one jar of crab apples from Mrs. William Lorman.

For the heroes there were dress swords and testimonial dinners, and for a convalescent Major Armistead a fine silver punch bowl of the exact dimensions of a thirteen-inch British bombshell. But he won far more than that. His wife Louisa presented him with a baby girl. Professionally, Madison sent him a spot promotion, and even better, he had that dream of every soldier—a little military fame. "So you see, my dear wife," he wrote Mrs. Armistead, "All is well, at least your husband has got a name and standing that nothing but divine providence could have given him, and I pray to my Heavenly Father that we may long live to enjoy."

Baltimore was already celebrating when a small sloop arrived on the evening of September 16, inched past the blockships, and docked at Hughes's Wharf between eight and nine o'clock. Released at last by Admiral Cochrane, the flag-of-truce packet was back with John S. Skinner, Francis Scott Key, and their elderly charge, Dr. Beanes.

Bystanders eagerly pumped them for news. What would the British do next? Well, said Key, the officers spoke of going to Poplar Island for repairs, then Halifax. Was Ross really killed? Yes, said John Skinner, no doubt about it. But the main focus of attention was Skinner's list of ninety-one prisoners held by the British fleet. All Baltimore was desperate for news of missing friends and relatives; now a great surge of relief swept the city.

Breaking away, the three new arrivals retired to the Indian Queen Hotel—but Francis Scott Key could not sleep. Vivid thoughts of the scenes he had witnessed raced through his mind. He had tried to express his feelings—the thrill of seeing the flag at dawn—in a few lines scribbled down right after the attack. Later he had added more during the long wait and sail back to Baltimore. Now these lines had jelled into a song, and he simply had to get it down on paper.

From the start, he almost certainly thought of it as being sung to the tune of "To Anacreon in Heaven," a familiar drinking song of the period. The same melody had already been borrowed in 1798 by Robert Treat Paine for a patriotic air called "Adams and Liberty," and Key himself had used it for an amateurish effort he composed in 1805 honoring the heroes of Tripoli.

---

*Skeptics have wondered how much Key could really see from his position eight miles down the Patapsco. From comments in the logs of nearby British ships, it seems clear that with the help of a spyglass he could easily watch the fort under fire.

Oddly enough, three years of research have unearthed only one first-hand account that refers to the flag without apparent knowledge of "The Star-Spangled Banner." It is the article by "R. J. B." (Midshipman Robert J. Barrett) of the British frigate *Hebrus*, appearing in the *United Service Journal*, April, 1841. Describing the squadron's withdrawal from Fort McHenry, Barrett recalled, "As the last vessel spread her canvas to the wind, the Americans hoisted a most superb and splendid ensign on their battery. . . ."

This raises an intriguing possibility. At the time Major Armistead bought the big flag from Mary Pickersgill, he also bought a smaller "storm flag," measuring seventeen by twenty-five feet, for $168.54. During the windy, rain-swept night of the bombardment, could he have substituted this storm flag and then, in the early morning, again hoisted his big flag in triumph as the British retired? Was it the storm flag, and not its famous counterpart, that Key actually saw?

Now it would do again, and he even went back, perhaps unconsciously, to some of the rhymes and images he had used nine years before. Taking a sheet of paper, he wrote it all out from beginning to end. Oddly enough, he gave it no title.

Next morning he showed it to John S. Skinner and also to his wife's brother-in-law, Judge Nicholson, free at last from the ordeal of Fort McHenry. One of them took or sent it to the offices of the Baltimore *American and Commercial Daily Advertiser* to be struck off as a handbill. Probably set by Samuel Sands, a fourteen-year-old printer's devil, copies were soon circulating throughout the city. A brief introduction explained how it came to be written, and a guideline gave the tune as "Anacreon in Heaven." But it mentioned no author and carried no title except the modest heading "Defence of Fort M'Henry." Weeks would pass before it became known as "The Star-Spangled Banner."

The song caught Baltimore's fancy right away. Key's words somehow conveyed perfectly the strange combination of fear, defiance, suspense, relief, and sheer ecstasy that went into that desperate night. The Fort McHenry garrison adopted it—every man received a copy—and the tavern crowds took it up. Resuming publication after a ten-day lapse, the Baltimore *Patriot and Evening Advertiser* ran it in full on September 20, proclaiming that it was "destined long to outlast the occasion and outlive the impulse which produced it."

It quickly spread to other cities, too, as the whole nation rejoiced in the news from Baltimore. Within a month, papers in towns as far away as Savannah, Georgia, and Concord, New Hampshire, were running Key's stirring lyrics. Everywhere they struck the right chord—the rare sense of exultation people felt about this totally unexpected victory.

For unexpected it was. As late as 7:15 A.M. on September 14 (fifteen minutes after Cochrane began his retreat), the vedettes at Elkton, Maryland, were warning the cities to the north that "the general opinion here is that Baltimore must fall." In Philadelphia crowds filled the streets all day, despite the rain, waiting for news that never came. Communications were out; the stage not running; the outlook bleak. Coming so soon after Washington, the situation had all the earmarks of another disaster.

And now the impossible had happened. Joy and relief swept the country: at Norfolk the *Constellation* fired rousing salutes; at Salem, Massachusetts, the town cannon boomed out in celebration. "Never have we witnessed greater elevation of public spirits," exclaimed the Salem *Register*. The triumph at Baltimore had erased all past impressions of the enemy's irresistible strength. "Ten thousand victories cannot give them their former hopes, and the spell is lost forever."

News of the British repulse at Baltimore caused a profound shock in London. Followed almost immediately by word of a disastrous defeat on Lake Champlain and the retreat of Sir George Prevost's invasion force from Plattsburg, New York, it forced British leaders to begin a sober reassessment of the war.

Gone were the harsh terms previously demanded by the British peace negotiators dickering with an American delegation at Ghent in Belgium. Faced with a seemingly endless war while unrest mounted at home and in Europe, Downing Street steadily relaxed its demands. Since the American negotiators had also retreated from their main demand, an end to impressment, soon there was little left to argue about. On Christmas Eve the treaty was finally signed, calling for a virtual return to the status quo before the war. The document was immediately ratified in London and forwarded to Washington for similar action there.

Across the Atlantic no one knew of these events as Admiral Cochrane went ahead with his plans for New Orleans. Reinforced by new regiments from England, the expedition reached the Gulf Coast by mid-December, and on the twenty-third it arrived on the banks of the Mississippi, less than eight miles below the city. The Americans under Major General Andrew Jackson were initially taken by surprise but reacted violently and blunted the British thrust.

Twice in the next nine days the British tried and failed to break Jackson's line; then a pause while they prepared a final all-out blow. Morale was helped by the arrival of a new military commander, Sir Edward Pakenham, sent out from England to replace the much-mourned General Ross. On January 8, 1815, all was set, and in the first light of day the British columns swept forward against the American defenses.

Andrew Jackson was ready. He had not been idle during the two weeks of preparation, and now a wall of earth, bristling with men and guns, barred the approach to New Orleans. The American line erupted in fire, shattering the advancing columns. Pakenham was killed; his second in command killed; a third general desperately wounded. By the time the attack was called off, the British had lost over two thousand men. In contrast, Jackson had only thirteen killed and thirty-nine wounded.

News of New Orleans reached Washington on February 4, and capping everyone's joy, on the fourteenth the peace treaty arrived from London. Madison lost no time in ratifying it, and on February 17, 1815, the United States and Great Britain were again at peace.

A surge of confidence swept America. It had many ingredients: there was Jackson's victory at New Orleans; the brilliant triumphs on Lake Erie and Lake Champlain; the splendid single-ship engagements on the open seas. But of them all, nothing did quite so much to pull the country together as that searing experience of losing Washington—the people's own capital—followed by the thrill of redemption when the same enemy force was turned back at Baltimore. In this swift turnabout new hopes were born, spirits raised, a nation uplifted. People forgot the dissension that had torn at the country through most of the war, and a new sense of national pride emerged.

This exciting excerpt is taken from Walter Lord's ninth book, The Dawn's Early Light, *recently published by W. W. Norton & Company. In this account of the War of 1812, the author harks back to one of his earliest interests—Fort McHenry—whose night of glory always intrigued him as a boy growing up in Baltimore. Six of Mr. Lord's nine books, including this new one, have been Book-of-the-Month Club selections or alternates; one,* A Night to Remember, *1955, was made into a successful movie, and another,* The Good Years, *1960, became a major television show. Mr. Lord tells us that he is the only man he knows of who spent 1971 with an 1814 calendar on his desk.*

Margaret Fuller

CONTINUED FROM PAGE 47

but in a letter to Emerson admitted the frightening truth: she had "only just escaped being drowned."

"*My* Italy," as Margaret exulted to Emerson, vital, sensuous Italy, was in 1847 divided into eight separate political states, with the temporal territories of the pope splitting the peninsula in half from sea to sea. Rome and the Papal States were ruled by the pope as a theocracy. The object of Mazzini's crusade was to unite all Italy into a single republic. In reaction, every frontier post of every state had standing orders for his immediate arrest.

Into this stewing caldron Margaret leaped as a devoted Mazzinian, eventually to become in Rome a letter drop for Mazzini's secret agents. She also bore introductions to various republicans, who were to help provide information for her *Tribune* dispatches. She began tepidly with a travelogue about Rome but quickly switched to politics, Holy Week, and Pope Pius IX. She questioned whether the newly elected pontiff would be able to fulfill his subjects' aspirations for desperately needed reforms—and whether he was as liberal as he seemed. This warning proved her among the most astute political observers in Europe. Time and again she would anticipate Pius's actions to an almost unbelievable degree.

But for Margaret, Holy Week had another and special significance. She had visited St. Peter's with the Springs and separated from them to view various chapels. Somehow there was confusion about their rendezvous, and she found herself alone. She was approached by an obviously cultivated young man, handsome, with flowing hair, a mustache, and melancholy eyes. He asked if he could be of any help. Margaret explained her situation, and he offered to find

a *carozza*—but no carriages were at hand. So he walked her to her lodgings. His name was Giovanni Angelo Ossoli.

He was, as it happened, eleven years her junior, the youngest son of a noble family important in the papal service. His mother had died when he was a child. His father was a high papal official; his three brothers served in the pope's *Guardia Nobile*, and one brother was, in addition, a secretary of the Privy Chamber. He himself was a marchese—heir of the great lords of the castle of Pietraforte. He was also secretly a republican, an admirer of Mazzini. Until the past two years almost nothing has been known in America about Ossoli. As late as 1963, Professor Miller could write that Angelo "on somewhat vague premises claimed to be a Marquis." Yet a superb Ossoli chapel, a symbol of the family's nobility, stands in one of the oldest churches in Rome for anyone to see.

Margaret thought at once that she had found another soul mate. But Angelo proved to be less ethereal and more real—as Margaret discovered when they picnicked with cheese and wine in the Alban hills. Nevertheless, from Margaret's letters it is evident that the relationship was still at this time platonic. Shortly, to her amazement, Angelo offered to marry her. She refused and left with the Springs for northern Italy.

Then the totally unexpected happened. Margaret parted with the Springs, and instead of resuming the homeward journey, as planned, hurried from Milan to Rome. Angelo, of course, was the magnet. Mickiewicz had written that she ought not to "leave your young Italian." Angelo himself had predicted to Margaret: "You will return—to me." Margaret said later, "I acted upon a strong impulse. . . . I neither rejoice nor grieve. I acted out my character." She had written,

"Woman is born for love, and it is impossible to turn her from seeking it." How well she knew herself!

Angelo was not in any sense an intellectual like the metaphysical transcendentalists. His book learning was meager, but he had the cultural education of any young man of the aristocracy, as was attested by Margaret's close friends in Rome, sculptor W. W. Story and his wife Emelyn. In no way was Angelo the "boor" that Hawthorne, who never met him, said he was. He was, curiously, anticlerical, but not anti-Catholic. He opposed only the Church's temporal power. Margaret found in him gentleness, sympathy, an intuitive understanding of her as a woman. He was able to provide the human warmth the Puritan moralists lacked. In short, she loved him, and unquestionably he loved her. He did not feel that the disparity in their ages was of any significance—though Margaret confided to a close friend that if someday he should love someone else, "I shall do all that this false state of society permits to give him what freedom he may need."

Their affair was kept secret from everyone—including, most especially, their families. Obliquely Margaret wrote to her mother: "I have not been so well since I was a child, nor so happy ever." In December of 1847 Margaret discovered that she was pregnant, and suddenly a dark mood of despair overwhelmed her. "At present I see no way out except through the gate of death," she wrote Caroline Sturgis, not yet confessing her condition. She continued to refuse Angelo's offers of marriage. "The connection seemed so every way unfit," she said. To Angelo such a marriage meant being disinherited, simply because Margaret was poor, Protestant, and radical. Indeed, until recently the Ossoli family took the view that Margaret ruined Angelo's life.

For all her depression Margaret

made no move toward abortion. When her girth could no longer be concealed, she sought a hiding place outside Rome, in the village of Rieti fifty miles distant. Since Angelo had volunteered as a sergeant in the popular "civic guard," he could not leave the city; and the two carried on an intense correspondence in Italian. Not the least of their problems was the papal censor. Angelo often hid secret messages in newspapers he sent to Margaret and used cover names in his letters. In many of their letters the personal and political are so intermingled as to become inseparable.

"I received this morning your dear letter," Angelo wrote. "The banker [a republican agent] sent a message that the documents didn't come, because Mazzini had escaped from Milano. I am very disturbed at hearing that you had such a bad night . . . I hope that you will always be courageous. I will be waiting for a sign to come straight into your arms, before they deprive us of even this pleasure. . . . Meanwhile I salute you, and believe me am always yours."

With the baby due in a fortnight, Margaret requested, "See if you can get details of Milano . . . I am terribly worried about our dear friends there [fighting against the Austrians]; how they must be suffering now! Also I am thinking much of you. I hope that you are less tormented. If we were together it would be a consolation, though everything is going badly now. But it's impossible to continue so, always, always. Goodby my love. I am sorry that we must pass so many days until you come; but I am glad I have the small portrait, which I look at often. M. (I hug you.)"

The baby, a boy, was born with difficulty September 5, 1848, and given its father's name and title, possible in Italy, then and now, even when the parents are not married. Angelo drew up a complex legal document in Latin on parchment. He was able to stay only one day, then rushed back to Rome. After several months the baby was placed in a foster home in Rieti, to Margaret's great distress; then reluctantly she took the diligence to Rome. She wished to hide the baby in the city, but Angelo refused, for fear their secret might become known. They continued, unwillingly, to live apart.

Margaret returned on the eve of one of the most stirring revolutions in European history, a dramatic upsurge of the Italian Risorgimento. With finances exhausted, she resumed at once her dispatches to the *Tribune*. She resumed, too, the systematic collection of material for the monumental *History of Italian Liberation* she proposed to write.

For her literary task Margaret had extraordinary sources of information. From Angelo's contacts she had access to the papal side; from Mazzini's contacts, the republican side. In addition, she herself had made noteworthy friends among the Italians, particularly the Marchesa Costanza Arconati Visconti (of the famed and ancient Visconti family). They carried on an active correspondence. And, fortunately, Lewis Cass, Jr., the American chargé d'affaires to the papal court, formed a strong liking for her and passed on much inside information. To top things off, she had chosen, accidentally, an apartment overlooking the pope's Quirinale Palace—so that she watched from her balcony some of the most dramatic scenes of the revolution.

One such scene occurred when the papal Swiss Guard fired on a crowd demonstrating for a constitution, civil rights, and redress of grievances. Inside the palace were Angelo's brothers, serving in the papal elite guard. Outside were Angelo and the civic guard. The crowd reacted with bedlam, setting fire to the great portal of the palace. Margaret saw "the broken windows, the burnt doors, the walls marked by shot, just beneath the loggia on which we have seen [the pope] giving the benediction."

A few days later Pius IX fled in the disguise of a simple priest, taking asylum with the Bourbon king of Naples, who also had a revolution on his hands. Events thereafter proceeded swiftly, with the entry of Mazzini and Garibaldi into Rome, the proclamation of a Roman Republic, and the advance of Bourbon, Spanish, Austrian, and French troops to destroy the Republic and restore the pope to his throne. Mazzini became chief of the Triumvirs governing the Republic and was in frequent contact with Margaret. (A number of his letters survive.) Garibaldi, whom Margaret had first seen while she was hiding in Rieti, became a leader in the defense of Rome—though alas for the Romans, not commander in chief.

The French army, sent by Louis Napoleon, was the first to arrive. The French soldiers were driven back and disorganized by Garibaldi but returned with reinforcements to besiege Rome. One of the defenders was Margaret's Angelo, now promoted to captain, in charge of a battery of rusty cannon. During the siege, from April 30 to July 4, 1849, Margaret was director of a military hospital, watching every cartload of wounded for the dreaded sight of Angelo. The last night of the attack she spent on the walls with Angelo, expecting death for them both. Today a *viale*—a tree-lined street —within the walls is named for her.

Margaret's dispatches to the *Tribune* were strictly factual. Nevertheless, in her editorial interpolations she called openly for United States recognition of the Roman Republic. In this she had the support of envoy Cass. But the State Department moved with such slowness that word of recognition did not arrive until a fortnight after the Republic's fall.

Margaret's partisanship for Mazzini did not blind her to the primary weakness in his revolutionary program—the lack of economic planning. With amazing insight for someone of her background, she commented: "Mazzini has a mind far in advance of his time in general, and his nation in particular. . . . And yet Mazzini sees not all: he aims at political emancipation; but he sees not, perhaps would deny, the bearing of some events which even now begin to work their way. . . . I allude to that of which the cry of Communism, the systems of Fourier, etc., are but forerunners." Margaret may well have already been aware of the 1848 publication by Marx and Engels of *The Communist Manifesto* and of its implications.

In spite of her criticism, her portrayal of Mazzini throughout is warm and deeply sympathetic, as her portrait of Garibaldi (whom at first she feared as a guerrilla bandit) is one of respect and admiration. It would be difficult to find in American journalism more graphic and moving descriptions than her eyewitness account of the tattered Garibaldi legion as it prepared to retreat to the hills and fight on for Italian freedom; or of Mazzini as he wandered hollow-eyed about the streets after the French had entered Rome.

The final paragraph of Margaret's last dispatch ended with a personal appeal: "O men and women of America, spared these frightful sights —acknowledge as the legitimate leaders and rulers those men who represent the people. . . ."

Angelo Ossoli, like Mazzini, escaped from Rome with an American passport provided by Cass at Margaret's request. Margaret and Angelo, both almost penniless, fled together to their child, hidden in Rieti. They found their "Nino" near death, emaciated by what was probably an intestinal infection. This added trauma very nearly threw Margaret into shock. She rallied and with Angelo's devoted help slowly nursed the baby back to life.

Angelo's father had died, and he was no longer on speaking terms with his brothers. He tried to recoup some of his inheritance but failed. Rieti, so close to Rome, was dangerous. In the autumn the dispirited revolutionaries moved on to Florence, where their American passports saved them from the Austrian police. There, according to a letter written in Italian by Angelo's sister Angela, Margaret and Angelo were married. This letter is the only evidence extant, and only in 1969 was it published in English. Margaret in fact became the Marchesa Ossoli.

Horace Greeley, apparently paying heed to rumors of free love, dropped Margaret from his payroll. Though her financial situation steadily deteriorated, she settled down to write her *History*. Angelo settled down to learn English. He had no way to earn a living. As Margaret wrote to Caroline Sturgis, "Being a nobleman is a poor trade in a ruined despotism."

Margaret revelled in her child, bathing, dressing, playing with him constantly, writing long letters to her friends about his graces. "Christmas day I was just up, and Nino all naked on his sofa, when came some beautiful large toys: a bird, a horse, a cat. . . . It almost made me cry to see the kind of fearful rapture with which he regarded them."

In Florence they lived quietly; among their few friends were the Brownings. Margaret had introduced them to the American public but reviewed Miss Barrett less favorably than Mr. Browning. Miss Barrett, in retaliation, initially proclaimed Margaret's situation scandalous and finally called her writings "naught." Also, she was wary of Margaret politically, "she being one of the out and out *Reds* and scorners of grades of society." Margaret, for her part, found Mrs. Browning "too gentle and faded at first sight to excite prospective feeling of any kind."

If such a buzz of gossip had been provoked in Florence, then what of America? To Emelyn Story, Margaret wrote that she did not admit "the rights of the social inquisition in the United States to know all the details of my affairs . . . many persons there will blame whatever is peculiar."

Everyone in the United States whom she had criticized or offended would be quick to condemn. Lowell already had mangled her in his *Fable for Critics*. Bishop John Hughes's reply to her dispatches had been to organize mass rallies in New York supporting Pius IX. Her praise of abolitionists had annoyed moderates. And finally, certain judgments in her dispatches had alienated many patriots: "My country is at present spoiled by prosperity, stupid with the lust of gain, soiled by crime in its willing perpetuation of slavery, shamed by an unjust war [the Mexican War], noble sentiment much forgotten even by individuals, the aims of politicians selfish or petty, the literature frivolous and venal. In Europe . . . a nobler spirit is struggling—a spirit which cheers and animates mine."

Increasingly it became evident that Ossoli, because of shrinking finances and more restive secret police, must leave Florence. So Margaret determined to take her husband, her child, and her manuscript to face the rigors of home. They chose the cheapest passage they could find—a merchant sailing ship, the *Elizabeth*. In mid-May, 1850, they embarked from Livorno. Margaret passed her fortieth birthday aboard ship, without celebration. Angelo was only twenty-nine.

A fortnight after sailing, as they reached Gibraltar, the captain died of smallpox. A week of quarantine, and the ship sailed on again, under command of the first mate. A few days later, little Nino developed smallpox. He did not die; Margaret, as before, nursed him back to life. On the eighteenth of July the first mate informed the passengers they would arrive in New York the following day. Margaret rejoiced and selected Nino's landing clothes. That evening the wind freshened, becoming a gale by midnight. The first mate, thinking they were off New Jersey, held course with close-reefed sails. In fact, they were off Long Island.

At 4 A.M. the *Elizabeth* struck a Fire Island sand bar. Through dawn and all morning the passengers and crew huddled in the forecastle while the ship gradually broke up from the relentless force of the waves and wind. The lifeboats had been smashed, and Margaret gave the only available life preserver to a sailor who went overboard to summon aid. Through the spray and rolling surf human figures could be seen on the beach; but they were beach pirates, waiting to pillage the wreck, and no help came. Toward midday the first mate abandoned ship with a wooden plank. "Save yourselves!" he shouted.

Margaret, with long dishevelled hair and still wearing her white nightgown, clung to her child and husband. She refused to make any attempt toward land without them both. She was last seen near the foremast just before a great wave struck.

Shortly before they sailed, Margaret had written that her life proceeded like a Greek tragedy—"I can but accept all the pages as they turn."

Of the three of them only the baby's body, cast up on the beach, was ever found.

Margaret's death was a public sensation, and an official investigation of the wreck was launched. From the New England group of Margaret's old friends, it was Thoreau, not Emerson, who rushed to Fire Island to seek in the sands any trace of Margaret's manuscript on the Roman Revolution. Nothing was discovered except a trunk containing Margaret's and Angelo's love letters and a few documents in Italian.

Even after her death, Margaret's psychic conflict with Emerson continued. Bleakly he noted in his journal, "I have lost in her my audience." He had repeatedly urged her to return to Concord; and when he was in Britain lecturing, he begged her to sail with him on the same ship. At the time Margaret received this letter she was in hiding and big with child. When news of Margaret's son and husband reached Concord, Emerson was gravely disturbed; he felt Ossoli had "taken her away" from him. Abruptly he changed his position. When Margaret asked advice on marketing her manuscript, he counselled her to remain in Italy while he acted as her agent. "It is certainly an unexpected side for me to support,—the advantages of your absenteeism," he wrote.

From their earliest meeting, Margaret had provoked him, saying such things as, "Your prudence, my wise friend, allows too little room for the mysterious whisperings of life." She called him "the cold stone." He replied defensively that she was like the "crackling of thorns under a pot." When, shortly after her death, he assumed—for whatever private reasons—the chief responsibility for assembling her memoirs, he confessed that Margaret "remained inscrutable to me."

He did not hesitate, however, to include remarks that he attributed to Margaret, attested to by no one but himself, which helped establish the false image of her overweening egotism, her "rather mountainous ME," as he described it. One such has passed into the history books: "She said to her friends, 'I now know all the people worth knowing in America, and I find no intellect comparable to my own.'" In the copy of the *Memoirs* owned originally by Margaret's first love, George T. Davis, pencilled beside this quotation of Emerson's is the phrase "Sublime bosh!"

Another example of his doctoring: Emerson stated in the *Memoirs* that Margaret's famous passage describing Mazzini was written to him—"You say, do I not wish Italy had a great man. Mazzini is a great man: in mind a great poetic statesman, in heart a lover, in action decisive and full of resources as Caesar. Dearly I love Mazzini, who also loves me." This paragraph in fact was not addressed to Emerson at all, but to Caroline Sturgis. Emerson deleted it from Caroline's letter and attached it to one addressed to him.

Emerson went further with his literary license. He revised Margaret's sentences and substituted words, modifying her lava-hot style into a semblance of his own stiff, pontifical language. He changed places and dates. He shifted copy from one source to another. He blue-pencilled, deleted, scissored whole sections of letters and journals. Sometimes letters were copied and originals discarded. Scores of pages of secret diaries were ripped away. In the end some vital part of Margaret had been amputated, and Emerson rested content with the portrait he and his fellow editors had created. In essence, despite their stated kindliness, they distrusted her because she was a woman intellectual who dared acknowledge her sexuality.

Even so, for all their labors, traces of the real Margaret Fuller could not be suppressed: the wide-ranging freedom of her mind and outlook, for one thing; and for another, her true, womanly, passionate hunger for love. A statement that Margaret once made tauntingly to Emerson could serve as a fitting epitaph for both Dear Waldo and herself: "You are intellect, I am life!"

Mr. Deiss is the author of The Roman Years of Margaret Fuller *(Crowell, 1969), a reinterpretation, based on new research, of this misunderstood woman.*

Boyhood

CONTINUED FROM PAGE 35

friends to be greeted, and new faces to be learned; there were not very many in either group, because the school after all was extremely small, but a pattern that seemed as timeless as the march of the seasons was resumed. The clanging of the academy bell, morning and evening, marked the familiar rhythm. It had always been like this —a decade and a half can be "always," to a teen-ager— and it would go on like this forever.

Yet there was an odd quality to that fall of 1915, when I began my final year in the academy. It was as if I stood aside, now and then, and watched the scene of which I was a part. The scene itself was permanent (as I supposed) but I myself was a transient, and suddenly I began to realize it. Boyhood was gone and youth itself would soon be over, and full manhood lay not far ahead. I was both impatient and reluctant. The eggshell was about to break, and although I wanted this to happen I was not sure that I was quite ready for it. It seemed important to get the last bit of flavor out of each moment, if only for the reason that nothing like this was ever going to happen again.

We had an acute sense of the impermanence of the present, and a haunting understanding that we were living for a time in a strange borderland between the real and the unreal, without enough knowledge of the country to tell one from the other. The daily routine, in study hall and classroom, was real enough, certainly; but so was the great flood of moonlight that sometimes lay on the countryside at night, turning the plain gravel road south into a white highway that wound through enchanted meadows across hills that might not be there at all when daylight returned. The reality of daily routine was going to vanish in a little while, and then it would be no more tangible than the neverland that bordered the moonlit roadway. Would memory be any more reliable than imagination? When both are forever out of reach, does what you once were count for more than what you once thought you might be? We live in dreams, and while we can we might as well make them pleasant ones.

Mostly they were. Yet there was something about our north country (or maybe it was something about me) that issued disquieting warnings now and then. There was the great emptiness off to the north, thousands of miles of it, with the cold tang of the ice age in the air; to the south was the land of the Mound Builders, whose best efforts produced nothing more than unobtrusive little scars on the earth; and all about us were the bleak acres of stumps, the dying towns, and the desolate farms that were being given up, discards in a game where most of the players had lost. Now and again these things demanded thought.

There was for instance one January morning that winter when Lewis Stoneman and I went sailing on skates. I do not know whether anyone does that nowadays, but it was quite a thing at the time and we had read about it in some magazine. You took thin strips of wood and made an oblong frame, about four feet long by three feet wide, added a couple of cross braces for stiffening and for handholds, and covered the frame with a piece of discarded bed sheet cut to size. Then you went to the ice, put on your skates, held the frame in front of you, and let the wind take charge. I talked about this with Lewis, who was a student at the academy and was for some reason known as Yutch, and it sounded like fun. We built the frames in the basement of Father's house, talked Mother into giving us a frayed old sheet, tacked pieces of it to the wood, got our skates, and one Saturday went down to Crystal Lake to see about it.

We were in luck. The lake had frozen late, that winter, and although the countryside was covered with snow there was little or none on the ice, which was smooth and clear as plate glass. Skating conditions were perfect, the sun was bright, the bare ice was like polished steel, and there was a brisk wind from the east—which was fine, because we were at the eastern end of the lake and the open ice stretched away to the west for more than eight miles. We put on our skating shoes, knotted the laces of our regular shoes together and hung them about our necks, got out on the frozen lake, held the sails in front of us, and took off.

The wind really was rather strong, blowing steadily and without gusts, and it filled our sails and took us down the lake at what seemed a fabulous speed. We had never moved so fast on skates before—had not imagined that it was possible to move so fast—and it was all completely effortless. All we had to do was stand erect, hold on to our sails, and glide away; it was like being a hawk, soaring effortlessly above the length of a ridge on an updraft of air, and it felt more like flying than anything that ever happened to me, later on in life, in an airplane.

Neither one of us knew anything at all about sailing. To tack, or even to go on a broad reach, was entirely beyond us; we had to go where the wind blew us, and that was that, and now and then I was uneasily aware that skating back against the wind, by sheer leg power, was going to be hard. However, there would be time enough to worry about that later. For the moment it was enough to soar along like thistledown, carried by the wind. The whole world had been made for our enjoyment. The sky was unstained blue, with little white clouds dropping shadows now and then to race along with us, the hills that rimmed the lake were white with snow, gray and blue with bare tree trunks, clear gold in places where the wind had blown the snow away from sandy bluffs, the sun was a friendly weight on our shoulders, the wind was blowing harder and we were going faster than ever, and there was hardly a sound anywhere. I do not believe I have ever felt more completely in tune with the universe than I felt that morning on Crystal Lake. It was friendly. All of its secrets were good.

Then, quite suddenly, came awakening. We had ridden the wind for six miles or more, and we were within about two miles of the western end of the lake; and we realized that not far ahead of us there was a broad stretch of sparkling, dazzling blue running from shore to shore, flecked with picturesque whitecaps—open water. It was beautiful, but it carried the threat of sudden death. The lake had not been entirely frozen, after all. Its west end was clear, and at the rate we were going we would reach the end of ice in a very short time. The lake was a good hundred feet deep there, the water was about one degree warmer than the ice itself, and the nearest land—wholly uninhabited in the dead of winter—was a mile away. Two boys dropped into that would never get out alive.

There was also a change in the ice beneath us. It was transparent, and the water below was black as a starless midnight; the ice had become thin, it was flexible, sagging a little under our weight, giving out ominous creakings and crackling sounds, and only the fact that we kept moving saved us from breaking through. It was high time, in short, for us to get off that lake.

Yutch saw it at the same moment I did. We both pointed, and yelled, and then we made a ninety-degree turn to the left and headed for the southern shore. If we had known how to use our sails properly the wind would have taken us there, but we knew nothing about that. All we could think of was to skate for the shore with all speed, and those sails were just in the way. We dropped them incontinently, and we never saw them again, and we made a grotesque race of it for safety, half skating and half running. We came at last to the packed floe ice over the shallows, galloped clumsily across it, reached the snow-covered beach, and collapsed on a log to catch our breath and to talk in awed tones about our escape.

We got home, eventually, somewhere along toward dusk. We at first thought we would skate back, but the wind was dead against us and skating into it seemed likely to be harder than walking along the shore; and besides we had had all of the lake we wanted for that day. We put on our other shoes and plodded cross-country through the snow, three miles to Frankfort, at which place, the afternoon train having left, we got a livery-stable rig to take us to Benzonia. (I am not sure Father altogether appreciated having to pay the liveryman the

required two dollars; he earned his dollars the hard way, and he never had very many of them. However, he paid up without a whimper.) We got home in time for supper—we ate that evening at Mother's table, and not in the academy dining hall—and when we were warm and full and rested we found that we had a great tale to tell, and told it, leaving my parents no doubt wondering just how much youthful exaggeration the tale contained. Actually, we had not so much as got our feet wet, and our escape had not been quite as narrow as we believed, but we had had an authentic glimpse over the rim and we did not like what we had seen; although, now that it was all over, it was fun to talk about it.

Yet the whole business cut a hard groove in my mind. I found after a while that I did not really want to talk about it. I did not even want to think about it, but I could not help myself. What I had seen through the transparent bending ice seemed to be nothing less than the heart of darkness. It was not just my own death that had been down there; it was the ultimate horror, lying below all life, kept away by something so fragile that it could break at any moment. Everything we did or dreamed or hoped for had this just beneath it. . . .

It all happened a great many years ago, and distance puts a deceptive haze on things remembered. As I look back on my final year in the academy I seem to recall the brief spring of 1916 as a time when life was extremely pleasant and singularly uneventful. The cataract might lie just ahead, but at the moment the river was lazy, without eddies or ripples. Europe was a long way off, and the echoes from its war reached us faintly, unreal and haunting, like the cries Canada geese make when they circle over Crystal Lake in the autumn, lining up the order of flight for their southbound squadrons. It was undeniable, of course, that we would very soon leave our little campus and go to whatever was waiting for us in the outside world, but that knowledge simply added a vibrant expectancy to life. Everything imaginable was going to happen very soon, but right at the moment nothing whatever was happening; if the time of waiting was almost over, its final moments had an uncommon flavor. Although we knew that we ought to think long and hard about what we were going to do, once the spring ripened into Commencement Week and then sent us off into unguided summer, most of the time we were quite undisturbed. The present moment was like a six-measure rest that had been mysteriously inserted into the score just as the composition was supposed to be coming to its climax.

Naturally, when I try to recall that time I remember hardly anything specific. I remember the spring sunlight lying on the campus, and the little academy buildings taking on dignity and looking as if they were going to be there forever—which, alas, they were not; I remember the band practice, and the orchestra practice, and the long, aimless walks we took on Sundays, tramping off the last vestiges of childhood, seeing things for the last time without realizing that it was the last time, unaware that once you leave youth behind, you see everything with different eyes and thereby make the world itself different. We would go across country to the power dam on the Betsie River, or along the shore of Crystal Lake to the outlet; and sometimes we went down the long hill to Beulah and then crossed the low ground to go up Eden Hill, a big shoulder of land that defined the horizon to the east . . . Eden Hill and Beulah Land, named by godly settlers for the Paradise where the human race got into the world and the Paradise it will enter when it goes out of it; or so people believed, although we lived then in the present moment and asked for no Paradise beyond what we had then and there.

From the summit of Eden Hill you could look far to the north and west, across the Platte Lakes to the limitless blue plain of Lake Michigan, with Sleeping Bear crouched, watchful, in the distance and the Manitou Islands on the skyline. Beyond the green wooded country to the east, hidden by the rolling easy ridges, was the little lumber town of Honor, and if we felt like making a really long walk out of it we could go on over to Honor, walk around the mill and its piled logs—they were still carving up some last allotment of first-growth wood there, although most of the county's mills were stilled —and then we could tramp the long miles home by way of Champion's Hill. This was a plateau which had been named half a century earlier by some Civil War veterans who made farms there; they had served in Sherman's corps in the Vicksburg campaign and something about the shape of this land reminded them of a great battlefield in that campaign and so they had put this Mississippi name in the heart of northern Michigan as a reminder of what they had seen and done. And we youngsters walked across it, all unthinking, on our way home to Sunday night supper.

Spring is a short haul in our part of Michigan, and we were kept fairly busy once the snow was gone making preparation for the exercises that would attend our graduation, which would be a great moment. For all that it was so small, Benzonia Academy crowded Commencement Week as full of events as the State University itself; and the graduating class was so small—just eleven of us, when fully mustered—that everybody had something to do. Which reminds me that by ancient custom, running back fully five years, the graduating class was supposed to present a play as the final event of its aca-

demic life. Our class elected to do something called "Peg o' My Heart," and of course nobody in the class had a vestige of acting ability, but somehow we got through the thing alive.

I remember practically nothing about the performance except that I was the leading man and, as such, was called upon by the script to kiss the leading woman, who was a most attractive classmate, just as the final curtain came down. Miss Ellis, who was directing the performance, made it clear that it would not be necessary or even permissible actually to kiss the girl; I could lay my hands gently upon her shoulders and incline my head slowly, and the curtain then would descend rapidly and action could be broken off with no casualties. I do recall that when the great night came and this portentous moment arrived we discarded Miss Ellis' instructions completely. I walked the girl home afterward so bedazzled by all that had happened that I was unable to muster the nerve to try to kiss her again. I think this puzzled her slightly, although I do not believe that she felt that she had missed anything much. Now that I think of it, she was the only member of the class I ever did kiss, it took what amounted to a convulsion of nature to bring that about, and there was no repeat performance. I suppose I was born for other things.

Fittingly enough, the class play was presented after all of the actors and actresses had ceased to be students at the academy. We were graduates, possessed of diplomas, the formal commencement exercises having taken place that morning, and technically we were out in the world on our own. I suppose I never would have kissed the leading lady if I had not realized that as a graduate I was no longer bound by Miss Ellis' instructions forbidding bodily contact. The commencement exercises had been painfully dignified, and whatever they may have meant to the audience I myself felt that they had been highly edifying. When I finally left the church, holding my rolled-up diploma like a field marshal's baton, I was full of high resolves and conscious rectitude, and I looked upon life from a loftier plane than I have ever occupied since.

This was all most impressive, and I recall the mood that possessed me as an odd blend of exaltation and humility; I knew so much, and I knew so little, and the world which I was about to enter did seem to be exceedingly complicated and unknowable. But above everything else it looked exciting. My time at the railway junction was ending, the morning limited was coming in and I was about to get aboard, and although I had no idea where it was finally going to take me I at least knew that everything was going to be very different from this time forward. The big adventure was beginning, even though I started it, I must admit, by walking down the hill to Beulah and going to work as a waiter-on-tables in the summer hotel there.

If I was marching forth to high adventure then, I had to begin by marking time. I was going to go to college; that had been determined long ago, and by virtue of a little money saved, more money borrowed, and arrangements to work for board and room once college was reached, everything was all set. But I could not go to college until the middle of September and this was only the middle of June, to spend the summer in idleness was inadmissible, and inasmuch as the job at the hotel would permit me to sleep at home while the hotel provided me with three meals every day, I could save almost every penny the waiter's job would bring in. So—down the hill, into the kitchen, on with the white coat and apron, and this is how you carry a loaded tray through a crowded dining room without dropping things on people's heads.

It all was most anticlimactic, no doubt, but it did not exactly seem so at the time. I was beginning to be independent, and although the independence was more apparent than real I was at least out of the house from dawn until dusk. If you have never been in control of any fragment of your life, to gain control even over a small part of it can be a heady experience; and to start off on the mile walk at daybreak, swinging down the hill before the town was awake, admiring Crystal Lake and the hills around it as the early light touched them, breathing the air that, essentially, had come drifting all the way down from northern Canada without once touching anything that would defile it, and to reflect while you were doing this that your boyhood at last was over and that every stride was carrying you nearer to man's estate—well, this was a moving and rewarding experience, even if it was totally undramatic. Life does not always need to be spectacular in order to be exciting.

We worked fairly hard. We were supposed to check in at six in the morning, and although there was a slack hour or two in midmorning and two or three hours that could be taken off in the afternoon we were not through for the day until eight at night, and when the dining room was full—as it usually was, in the middle of the summer—the work was fairly hard. However, it could have been much worse. There was a sort of dormitory, back of the hotel, for such waiters as did not live at home, and in the afternoon we could all go in there, change to bathing suits, and then walk down the lawn to Crystal Lake and take a swim, which was enough to make up for any sort of drudgery. Now and then, on the beach, we would encounter young women who were guests at the hotel, and we could lounge and chat with them, and accompany them into the water, just as if we were not waiters at all.

As a matter of fact girls did not claim much of our attention that summer. We had no time for them, except for those afternoon recess periods, and we usually spent that time swimming, followed by a quick visit to Terpening's pavilion for ice cream, without bothering to see who was available on the beach. Actually we worked rather hard, seven days a week, and the pay scale began and ended with a weekly wage of five dollars. We were allowed to keep all tips, which helped, but our guests were not lavish in that respect and many of them left no tips at all, so we did not make very much money.

However, we did not really expect to. If we could lay by a few dollars during the summer we were just that much ahead of the game; and besides, at that time and place the going wage for adult labor, unskilled or semi-skilled, was fifteen cents an hour. Prices of course were a great deal lower than they are now, but they were never low enough to make that kind of pay scale anything but bad. The men who worked for such wages were getting angry and their anger was becoming visible, even to me. I learned that summer, to my bewilderment, that even our own Benzie county—a bucolic section of the unstained Michigan countryside if ever there was one—had developed quite a number of outright Socialists, and although I occasionally read about Socialists I had not expected actually to see any, especially not this close to home. (They were much in the minority, of course, but their numbers were fairly impressive when the county's limited population was taken into account.) Men could be seen reading Eugene Debs's "Appeal to Reason" quite openly; men who lounged on their doorsteps in sweaty undershirts, gnawing at the stems of corncob pipes, not at all the sort of men who went to our church on Sunday to listen to Mr. Mills. It was disturbing to have avowed Socialists right in our midst, and nobody seemed to know what to make of it.

Father would assuredly have had a word for me if I had told him about my state of mind. He was no Socialist, but he knew what these men were angry about and he thought they were right to be angry; in point of fact he was angry too, not because he himself had to work for a genteel-poverty income, but because he believed that greed, oppression, and injustice (visible now and then even in the idyllic forests of Michigan) were threatening to destroy everything that America stood for. Whether he realized it or not, he was looking for a broader field than the principal's office at Benzonia Academy offered him. He had abundant energy, he could write and speak with genuine eloquence, and he had an eye that could see, and he wanted to use these qualities for something a little more significant than providing artificial respiration for a little school that almost certainly would not survive him. I did not at the time realize that he was going through anything like this.

Father was a dedicated Theodore Roosevelt man, a

card-carrying member of the Bull Moose Party. He had campaigned for Roosevelt, on the village and county level, in 1912, and in 1916 he had been elected a delegate to the national convention of the Progressive Party, and down to Chicago he went, to see the great leader in person and get inspiration for the approaching Presidential election.

What he got, of course, was profound disillusionment. Like hundreds of other delegates, he had keyed himself up (in Roosevelt's own words) to stand at Armageddon and to battle for the Lord, and these were words he could rise to because he was both a devout Roosevelt man and a good Biblical scholar. But the emotional build-up led to nothing but a letdown. Roosevelt was not going to run for President after all, the Progressive Party had served its purpose and would be dismantled; instead of standing at Armageddon, rallying to a great banner held high in a clanging wind, they were to go home quietly, vote for Charles Evans Hughes, and resume their places in the Republican Party which they had spent four years learning to distrust. They had been let down, and it was too much. Father never said much about it, but I am convinced that in the fall of 1916, for the only time in his life, he voted the Democratic ticket. Woodrow Wilson—precise, professorial, full of hard passions but apparently having no zest for living—might seem an unlikely heir for the Bull Moose legacy but he got a lot of Bull Moose votes that fall.

Father brought back from Chicago deep emotions that should have been discharged there and were not, and I think this helped to pull him out of the job he had trained himself for. From the classroom and the pulpit he had fought against ignorance, and against that combination of self-indulgence, ill will, and stupidity that people of his generation called sin, and now it was time to do something else. He had not gone into the Progressive Party just because Roosevelt's mighty personality had overwhelmed him; he had been headed in that direction for a long time. I suppose he could be called a Populist, although I do not think he would have applied that term to himself, and anyway by this time it has become too vague to mean very much; it is applied nowadays to practically anyone who flourished after 1885, lived west of the Alleghenies, and stood somewhat to the left of Grover Cleveland. An idea of the direction his thoughts had been taking is provided by a Fourth of July speech which he made in some small town in Michigan either in 1906 or 1907.

The speech began conventionally enough by paying tribute to the heroes of 1776 and making proper mention of Lexington, Concord, Saratoga, and Yorktown, but it did not go on to let the eagle scream in the traditional Fourth of July manner. It remarked that we look back on the past in order to find courage and inspiration to face the immediate future and that the Revolutionary War was fought to defend a declaration of principles which became "the rallying cry for the oppressed of every land." The battles of that war were the battles of all mankind, and the spirit that led men in '76 would yet be "the vital, potent force that shall astonish and overthrow domestic greed as completely as it once did a foreign tyrant."

He did not leave "greed" as a vague generality that could mean as much or as little as anyone chose. To the best of his ability he spelled it out; in the manner, to be sure, of the early 1900's rather than the 1970's. He was talking about monopoly, about the "spirit of selfish individualism" which inspired monopoly, about the unreachable corporations which practiced "a great system of extortion," drove prices up under cover of a fraudulent protective tariff, kept wages down by importing whole shiploads of Europe's "pauper labor" against whose handiwork the tariff was supposed to be an essential bulwark, and used the vast powers of finance to exert an increasing control over the law, the press, and the school in such a way as to make reform almost impossible.

"Whenever a man is found wise enough and brave enough to denounce these archconspirators against the people's liberties," he continued, "they accuse him of assailing the sacred rights of property and of being in league with anarchy." This outcry rallied the "honest respectable element" in every community—the frugal farmer, worker, merchant, and professional man who had worked hard to save a competence for a rainy day—and ironically led them to defend "the very vultures that are gorging upon their vitals."

This of course was the jargon of old-line Populism, a shotgun charge aimed at the forces whom Roosevelt himself could only denounce as malefactors of great wealth, but there are two things to be said about it. First of all, this was not the spread-eagle Fourth of July bombast with which glib speakers of that era prodded at receptive rural patriotism; and beyond that it was an odd way for a small-town schoolmaster to be talking. The man who put that speech together, and then stood in the bandstand of a village park and delivered it before a sunbaked audience that was there half out of curiosity and half out of a sense of duty, was a man with something on his mind and with a determination to have his say about it. Obviously, he believed that he saw something taking America by the throat and threatening to choke out, if not its very life, at least its life-giving spirit.

Feeling so, he believed that to break this grip would be of service to all mankind. He had his full share of that profound conviction which lies so close to the headwaters of the American spirit: the conviction that if in the end the world is saved from disaster the saving will be done in America and by Americans. As a people whose ideas about the cosmos have at least in part an Old Testament base, we have a deep suspicion that we are the chosen people. We may not actually be the ones specifically mentioned in Scripture, but we feel that we are fairly close; maybe Providence made a supplementary choice somewhere along the way. (After all, no less a man than Abraham Lincoln, trying to nerve his countrymen for the shock of civil war, spoke of them as the almost chosen people.) This feeling is in fact one of the most powerful forces in American life, and now and then it leads to interesting happenings. It frequently makes us hard to live with, and it bewilders a great many people—including, often enough, ourselves. For every so often it impels us to take drastic action, and a subconscious belief in mission is not always accompanied by the good sense to make a sound choice of the sort of action that is required. Sometimes we act with wisdom and at other times we do not. The same impulse that led us to destroy Hitler's obscenely contrived Nibelungen Reich, composed in equal parts of the fantasies of Teutonic chivalry and grisly shapes from the heart of darkness, led us a few years later into Southeast Asia, where we have made obscene contrivances of our own.

But whether we act wisely or foolishly, we always feel that what we do is important to the whole wide world and not just to ourselves, and the responsibility runs all the way down to the conscience of the individual. We are mindful of the text which, telling the chosen ones that they were the salt of the earth, asked what the world would do if the salt ceased to be salty. A man who feels so will make no small decisions. Thus it happens that the elderly principal of an unimportant school in one of the remote parts of the earth, reflecting that time was short and anxious to make good use of the thin years that remained to him, might conclude that he owed to mankind a larger debt than he had yet tried to pay. What he did might mean nothing to anybody in particular, but by what he was and what he believed he would do it as if the fate of the world depended on it. By the end of the summer of 1916, I am sure, Father had made up his mind to leave the academy.

Of all of this I at that time knew nothing. I was thinking about myself, and about the great things that lay ahead of me; the place that had been all the world was about to become nothing more than a receding milestone, growing ever smaller with increasing distance but not really changing. The institution that had shaped me (and in a sense it was simply an extension of my own home) would remain just as it always had been: always, that is, for the last ten or twelve years. Changes that took place would happen to me, not to what I left behind. My background was immutable, and when I finally went off to Oberlin I felt no need to take a fond backward glance.

A college freshman was as far from maturity then as he is today, but it did seem to me that I was just about grown up. Boyhood certainly was ended. Youth indeed remained, to be squandered as blithely as if it came from an inexhaustible fountain, but the mere fact that I could be prodigal of it if I wished made a difference. I felt that by getting to college, exchanging a small campus for a large one, I was being set free.

That was something of an exaggeration, considering the Oberlin of 1916; there were innumerable laws against all known forms of misconduct, and they were enforced with ferocious rigor. Fraternities, for instance, were outlawed; and in that same fall of 1916, just before the college year opened, it was learned that practically the entire football squad had formed, and gave allegiance to, a secret fraternity. The entire football squad, accordingly, was thrown out of college without further ado, and a pickup team that was hastily organized with untaught volunteers, who went nobly forth to slaughter for the honor of the school, took a fearful beating every Saturday of the season; I believe Ohio State, which was just then emerging to big-league status, beat Oberlin by 128 to nothing.

The college authorities, in other words, meant what they said, and they could be grim. And yet (to repeat) I was at least away from home, and I felt that I had freedom. One autumn evening, greatly daring, I went with another boy to the nearby city of Elyria, walked uncertainly into a saloon, and drank a glass of beer, after which we slunk out, boarded an interurban, full of the consciousness of guilt and high adventure, and went hastily back to Oberlin. Never have I committed a sin that was as pleasurable and as exciting.

All of this, to be sure, is beside the point. Benzonia Academy was my fixed point of reference, and everything that happened to me was to be compared with what had happened in Benzonia. This put an unusual gloss on commonplace adventures, now and then, so that the innocent little trip to Elyria seemed like a weekend lost around Sodom and Gomorrah; but it did no harm, and I had a deep affection for the place which, in a way, had seemed so repressive. The academy would always be there, and some day I would return, probably as a famous foreign correspondent on furlough, and tell the impressionable young people graphic tales about gathering the news in places like Paris and London.

The one thing I did not dream of at that time was that the academy was not going to wait for me. My own class of 1916 was second from the last class ever to be graduated there. At the end of the 1917 school year

Father resigned his post, and one year later, in the summer of 1918, the academy closed its doors forever. Barber Hall was torn down a few years later; it was a fire hazard, a place subject to being broken into by rowdies, and a building of no conceivable use. The boys' dormitory, which had been a rambling collection of gable ends stuck together almost at haphazard, was cut to pieces and the pieces were taken away to make dwelling places. And the girls' dormitory, on the first floor of which our family had lived for several years, was turned into a village community house. It survives to this day, a most serviceable old building, looking rather hollow-eyed because its upper floors are boarded up and present blank, uncurtained windows to the public gaze. It has been in existence for well over half a century, and less than a decade of its life was devoted to the function for which its builders intended it. Nothing less dramatic than this building's story, and nothing less important than the death of the academy which had built it, could easily be imagined. But in an almost unnoticeable way the affair marked the closing of an era.

A graduate of the academy, meeting Father in the fall of 1918, asked him why the academy had disintegrated. Father replied that any small, undernourished institution of that sort was simply the reflection of one man's activity: when the man ceased to be active the institution ceased to exist. Whether he was consciously adapting Emerson's remark that an institution is the lengthened shadow of one man or worked the thought out for himself I do not know, but he had the right explanation. Benzonia Academy, founded by dedicated men to light an educational lamp in a wilderness which, left to itself, would remain in darkness, had outlived the condition that called it into being. The wilderness had been destroyed, and without exactly meaning to, the men who destroyed it had let in the light. The academy had become an anachronism. Once it existed because a state needed it and a community willed it; in the end, no longer really essential, it existed because one man willed it. When America went to war in the spring of 1917 he focused his will on another objective. It took the academy just a year to die.

A new era was beginning, and if the academy had not quite prepared us to understand it, the same can be said of every other school on earth. No one was prepared, anywhere, and the deeper we get into this new era the more baffling it becomes. All that seems clear is that the mind of man now is obliged to adjust itself (without loss of time, and under penalty of death) to the greatest revolution in human history; a revolution, not in the relations of class with class and society with society, but in the nature of man's idea of the universe and of his place in it. We have won a fight that we ought to have lost; which is to say that we control the world we live in, and its levers are in our hands even though we have no idea what to do with them. We can go anywhere and do anything, and because the fabulous machine we have created can neither be reversed, put in neutral, or turned aside we have to go and do to the utmost limit, which is as likely as not to be our own destruction. Not since he came down out of trees and lost his tail has man been compelled to make such an adjustment in his ways of thinking. The breaking of horizons that took place in the Renaissance was a false dawn in comparison. He is headed now, infallibly, for the infinite . . . in either direction.

The academy in fact had done as well as it could, and if it left with some of its students the idea that what they do here should be done with an eye on its eternal consequences—well, a man going out into the twentieth century could be given worse advice.

When America went to war Father saw the war through Woodrow Wilson's eyes and heard the summons in Wilson's voice; if Roosevelt, in the showdown, had failed to call him to Armageddon, Wilson sounded the call and Father responded. He left the academy to support the great cause as a free lance, believing that his eloquence and his knowledge of world history ought to be of service. His knowledge of world history was limited and may have led him at times to unsound judgments; but men in a position to know far more than he knew did no better with what they knew, and all in all he did a good, serviceable job. He wrote analytical articles for various Michigan newspapers, and he set up a series of lectures explaining the causes and the meaning of the war and travelled up and down the state delivering them to a considerable variety of audiences. These talks seem to have gone over well in the high schools—an enthusiastic educator in Saginaw wrote that they "should be presented in every high school in the United States"— and a former academy student, finding himself early in 1918 wearing khaki with other trainees at Camp Custer, was marched with his battalion into the mess hall one day to listen while Mr. Catton explained the true significance of the war. He had one lecture on "spiritual conscription" designed for church groups, explaining how Christians could sustain the young men who were being taken into the army; and in a notebook wherein he jotted down points to be made in his talks he scribbled this sentence: "The one inevitably oncoming thing, in politics, industry, commerce, education and religion, is *Democracy*."

All of this, of course, was a venture that had no tomorrow. He had cut loose from his job and had in fact destroyed the base on which the job had rested, and once the war was over nobody was going to want articles or speeches about why we fought and why we had to win. Furthermore, he was 62 years old, and his prospects in a postwar job market were not good. Presumably he was well aware of this, and privately, where no one could hear him, he did a little whistling for his courage's sake. In his notebook there is a yellowed newspaper clipping, worn by much handling: a little poem entitled "At Sixty-Two," which apparently he had read a great many times. One stanza gives the tone of it:

> *Just sixty-two? Then trim thy light*
> *And get thy jewels all reset;*
> *'Tis past meridian, but still bright,*
> *And lacks some hours of sunset yet.*
> *At sixty-two*
> *Be strong and true,*
> *Scour off thy rust and shine anew.*

Excellent words, but it did not lack as many hours of sunset as might have been thought. For a long time Father had suffered an abdominal pain, with certain distressing symptoms, which he did his best to ignore. But some time early in 1919 the matter reached a point where it could be ignored no longer, nor could it be concealed. He confided, at last, in a doctor, and learned (as I suppose he had expected to learn) that he had cancer, and that although an operation would presently be performed it was not likely to do much good. His number, in other words, was up, and now there was

nothing to do but get his affairs in order, compose his mind, and wait for the end.

. . . Old age, as I said before, is like youth in this one respect: it finds one waiting at the railroad junction for a train that is never going to come back; and whether the arrival and possible destination of this train is awaited with the high hopes that youth entertains when it waits for its own train depends, no doubt, on the individual. I think Father had hopes.

But you know how it can be, waiting at the junction for the night train. You have seen all of the sights, and it is a little too dark to see any more even if you did miss some, and the waiting room is uncomfortable and the time of waiting is dreary, long-drawn, with a wind from the cold north whipping curls of fog past the green lamps on the switch stands. Finally, far away yet not so far really, the train can be heard; the doctor (or station agent) hears it first, but finally you hear it yourself and you go to the platform to get on. And there is the headlight, shining far down the track, glinting off the steel rails that, like all parallel lines, will meet in infinity, which is after all where this train is going. And there by the steps of the sleeping car is the Pullman conductor, checking off his list. He has your reservation, and he tells you that your berth is all ready for you. And then, if he is like all other Pullman conductors, he adds the final assurance as you go down the aisle to the curtained bed: "I'll call you in plenty of time in the morning."

. . . in the morning.

Bruce Catton stands beside the simple Civil War monument in Benzonia—made by men, he says, "who built it with their own hands because they could not pay for a professional job. The spirit that built it redeems it; it stands today as the most moving, heartwarming Civil War memorial I ever saw."
DANIEL KRAMER

Viking America

CONTINUED FROM PAGE 29

stories of how they came to be here among new peoples. He has, in short, become an American.

But the suppositions bringing the Vikings directly into the mainstream of American history are those regarding Columbus. Enterline frankly admits that it is impossible to show any direct, *noncircumstantial* evidence that Columbus himself had any knowledge of Norse activities on the western mainland. But many of Columbus' contemporaries seem clearly to have had such information. Since much of history is based on circumstantial evidence, it is fair to pay attention to circumstantial evidence in this case also. Enterline argues as follows:

. . . all writers on the subject of Columbus have been curious and dissatisfied about the explanation of Columbus' motivation for his voyage. If his belief that he could reach Asia by sailing westward was based on nothing more than the generally accepted knowledge that the earth was round, it could not possibly have received the interest and backing it did. . . . But the scholars of his time were quite right in opposing Columbus' scheme to sail westward to Asia, because they knew the size of the globe and the safe maximum time at sea for a fully provisioned ship. There was absolutely no hope of Columbus' sailing even one third of the actual distance westward to Asia. . . . In the absence of *sure* knowledge of *something* out there, Columbus' project appears to be either that of a god or a naive self-deceiver who was saved by good luck. Those writers who have tried to understand Columbus in more human terms have generally come to the conclusion that he had shadowy information of which we are no longer aware, based on the actual existence of the American continents, but misconstrued as the east coast of Asia.

An important part of the author's circumstantial approach is to show that such shadowy information was not held uniquely by Columbus but was widely shared. Indeed, Enterline points out that in the early fifteenth century

academic interest in a westward view of eastern Asia increased markedly. . . . This occurred just during the time when [many former believers in a flat world] were being converted to a Ptolemaic theory which forced them to think quantitatively in terms of the entire globe. The result, aided and abetted by Ptolemy's own incorrectly small estimate of the size of a degree and by a longing for Marco Polo's spice islands, was an increasing pressure for downward revision of the concepts of the size of the Earth. It was this revision, necessarily incorrect, which was responsible for getting America "officially" discovered. Within a short time, people like Doctors Paolo Toscanelli [1397–1482] and Hieronymus Müntzer [1437–1508] began discussing the practical possibility of making an actual voyage westward to Asia. From the number of different official proposals to kings on record, it is not difficult to imagine how many less official schemes went unrecorded. Neither is it difficult to imagine that unrecorded actual attempts were made. . . . The first downward rationalizations of the size of the degree sufficient to force the east coast of Asia to coincide with the east coast of America . . . seem to have been arrived at by Columbus. However, it would be doing him a dishonor to suggest that such a fantastic rationalization was not already in the air. It would seem that only definite knowledge of land which could not otherwise be accounted for would have called for such mental gymnastics. These rationalizations were eventually able to overcome the objections of royal advisers, and soon thereafter the necessary funding for what was to be the official discovery of America became available.

It was the vague information on the Norse dispersal and the resulting belief that eastern Asia was so close to the West, according to Enterline, that caused Columbus and his contemporaries to re-estimate downward their idea of the size of the globe, and hence of the degree, and then turn around and use this reduced value as an argument for the

practicality of sailing westward themselves to Asia. The sources of the shadowy European information on the Norse dispersal are bound to be vague, especially since recognized European communication with the Greenland settlements terminated in 1408. But evidence such as European garments from the *late* fifteenth century found in a Greenland graveyard shows that unrecognized, unofficial communication *did* continue. Much of that communication may have been maintained by pirates known to have attacked Greenland in that era and by clandestine private traders from Bristol, England.

The author now takes another tack:

. . . Columbus' contemporary Las Casas evidently interviewed Indians in Cuba and found that 'The neighboring Indians of that island asserted that there arrived to this Island of Hispaniola other bearded white men like us, not many years before us.' He recorded this in connection with the story of a lost pilot who supposedly preceded Columbus, but the beards could just as well have been worn by Norsemen as by Spanish conquistadores. . . . If these men had somehow also encountered the Aztec/Mayan civilizations in nearby Yucatan, or even heard about them through the Cubans, and returned the information to Europe, then one might be able to explain why Marco Polo's extravagant lands of gold began, as with one Albertin de Virga's 1415 map, to be associated with the West instead of the East. Before 1400, Zeno told a story of gold-users south of the Norse countries which would certainly have hastened the process as well. These stories provide a refutation to the proclamation by some scholars that Columbus could not have been motivated by the Norsemen, because he sailed so far south. If such information, in whatever form and by whatever means, reached Columbus, then it would be not at all surprising that the course he plotted for the golden land of Cathay led him eventually to the latitudes of the Aztecs. Those who wish to may imagine Dominicus Ducier's 1422 map, which shows continental land in the western ocean, as extending to those latitudes, and a scholar of the stat-

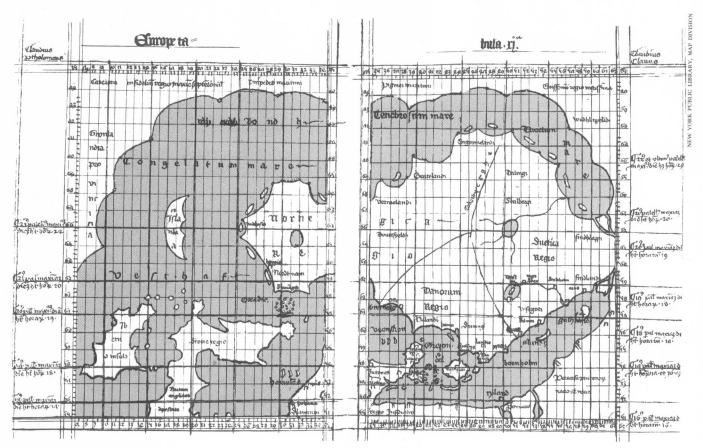

The cartographic evidence for Enterline's theory rests largely on reinterpreting old maps. Above, for example, is a map claiming to show Scandinavia, made in 1427 by a Dane named Claudius Clavus. It resembles Scandinavia not at all; but when a simplified version of this map is juxtaposed with a modern sketch map of Alaska's Seward Peninsula (right), a striking similarity of outline is quickly visible. Enterline's suggestion is that valid Norse information about northwestern North America was misconstrued and applied, through the "Grand Misunderstanding," to what was taken for Scandinavia.

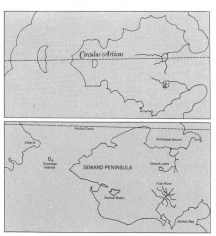

JAMES R. ENTERLINE

ure of [Armando] Cortesão has taken a nautical chart of 1424, which introduced new islands in the western ocean, to represent these very West Indies. The medieval Norsemen tell us in several texts that they believed Vinland was connected with Africa. They may, in saying this, have been letting us know how far south they had gone. Indeed, if North America was taken to be Asia, then South America fits the geographical situation of Africa very accurately. . . . This analogy would have been the ultimate step of the Grand Misunderstanding, equating the entire New World with the entire Old World.

The "Grand Misunderstanding" is an entirely new concept invented by Mr. Enterline to explain how Columbus and his contemporaries could have been influenced by Norse information without the fact being explicitly recorded by history. In effect, it amounts to a failure by the Norse explorers and all those who heard about the Norse explorations to realize that the American land was a new continent rather than the eastern edge of Asia. But the full concept of the Grand Misunderstanding involves a much wider geographic region than the eastern seaboard and calls for a revolution in the study of historical cartography. Enterline claims that pre-Columbian Old

World maps show in several cases, for example, an island at the northeastern corner of the Eurasian continent (Siberia) whose outline is similar to the island at the northeastern corner of North America, Baffin Island; islands along the arctic coast of Eurasia that look very much like the arctic archipelago north of Canada; and peninsulas at the north-

107

western corner of Eurasia (Scandinavia) that look just like the peninsulas of the northwestern corner of North America, i.e., Alaska. In other words, the Norse explorers who made these regional maps, which eventually found their way into the hands of European cartographers, thought they were exploring Eurasia, from east to west. One of the more famous maps involving this misconception is Claudius Clavus' 1427 map of "Scandinavia," which is actually a much better representation of Alaska's Seward Peninsula than of any part of Scandinavia. The extent of the explorations implied thereby is certainly greater than anything heretofore proposed, but it seems to be supported by the wide variety of archaeological and anthropological evidence existing along the route of the Northwest Passage.

A noncartographic occurrence of the Grand Misunderstanding seems to have arisen when Europeans heard stories of the Eskimos migrating eastward into Greenland. The Eskimos, who had started their migration in Alaska, described themselves in Greenland as having come from the western end of the continent, at the northern corner. Europeans hearing this decided that they meant they were from Lapland, in northern Scandinavia, and had travelled eastward in northern Asia. Meanwhile, the Europeans reasoned, the Norsemen had sailed westward to Greenland and met the presumed Laplanders there, supposedly just off the northeastern corner of Asia. Thus Claudius Clavus thought the Eskimos were Karelians from near the White Sea.

Another kind of misunderstanding confirms the idea that maps were indeed supplied by Norsemen to European cartographers. This misunderstanding, committed by cartographers rather than explorers, is called by Enterline the "Smaller Misunderstanding." A cartographer committing the Smaller Misunderstanding decided that if a map of an unknown land (and Scandinavia was an unknown land, cartographically, in pre-Columbian times) came to him *from Scandinavian hands*, then it must be *a map of Scandinavia*. There are many Old World maps, otherwise relatively accurate, in which the representation of Scandinavia looks nothing like the actuality of that region, but does look like, for example, Baffin Island, the Canadian Arctic Archipelago, and even the entire Quebec-Labrador peninsula.

The author has admitted that he cannot show any evidence proving that Columbus himself knew directly about the Norse explorations. But he does arrive at this conclusion: "There was an unquestionable *indirect* influence of fundamental proportions on Columbus, through the vague but persistent ideas of land in the West which were already in the air. The great accomplishment by Columbus was to make the Grand Misunderstanding become accepted throughout the rest of the European scholarly world."

The possibility that such misunderstood information about Norse explorations could have lain under the noses of historians for centuries without being noticed motivated Enterline to search out facsimiles or originals of nearly every known world map from the Middle Ages and early Renaissance and to examine them for possible evidence of such misunderstandings. He found that dozens of such maps contained strange lands that previous historical cartographers had dismissed without analysis as figments of medieval cartographers' imaginations but that were actually examples of the Grand or Smaller misunderstandings. The author's method, after recognizing the existence also of medieval textual documents incorporating such misunderstandings, was to arrange all the ninety-odd documents involved into a chronological sequence and

then to study the historical developments reflected in that sequence. The results led to the theory of a dispersal of the Greenland settlements westward into Eskimo America and southwestward into Indian America in the century immediately preceding Columbus.

My own first contact with James Robert Enterline was in the fall of 1965, when he began frequenting the New York Public Library's Map Division, of which I am chief. The author of this book is, surprisingly, a mathematician—he formerly administered a successful computer-technology company and has designed a computer for the United States Air Force. But he was stirred by Yale University's announcement of the Vinland Map in 1965 to turn to full-time research on the Norse question. He brought his objectivity as a scientist to bear on the highly partisan question of Columbus versus Leif Eiriksson, and a new theory resulted that is even more startling than any theory either partisan faction had previously imagined. Perhaps this kind of author, combining a mathematician's attention to detail with the fresh approach of a convert to a new subject, was what was required to produce the insightful and revolutionary synthesis that *Viking America* is. Enterline made field trips to Greenland and Iceland, and he has done documentary research in the British Museum as well as in the major collections in the United States. His present scholarly role was affirmed last fall when he was invited to address the annual meeting of the Society for the History of Discoveries held at Yale University.

The author approached me in the fall of 1966 because he had difficulty believing the unexpected implications into which his own research was leading him, and he sought a critical estimation from me. Hours of discussion led to what amounted to an encouragement on my part, for

I felt he was on the threshold of making some startling discoveries.

The eight-hundred-page manuscript he finished several years later, however, is not the book discussed here. The present book is a distillation for a less cartographically specialized spectrum of readers and summarizes the cartographic chronological analysis while giving complete details of the conclusions based on that analysis. Specialists wishing to pursue the painstaking details of the maps will have to await release of this supportive evidence in another volume. I have read the manuscript of that volume and find that each document discussed is supplied with an individual bibliography, that it contains a separate bibliography of facsimile atlases, and that it contains a general bibliography which, together with the one in the present volume, embodies by far the most comprehensive and up-to-date collection of references on the Viking presence in America ever assembled in English. In short, the research on

Dr. Alexander, who is chief of the Map Division of The New York Public Library, has particular interest in the cartography of the Age of Discovery.

which the present book is based is thorough and dependable.

There is no question but that *Viking America* introduces many ideas that are bound to provoke discussion. If these ideas can withstand the scrutiny of scholars, they will have introduced a wholly new aspect into the mainstream of American history.

Of Forks & Conformity

As Speaker of the House of Representatives in the late 1890's, Thomas B. Reed of Maine was known as Czar Reed for his rather dictatorial manner of conducting House affairs. At the center of his public philosophy was his conviction that leadership, while it might sometimes influence, was in reality only a reflection of the public will. Speaking on this theme at Colby College in 1885, he remarked:

Whoever invented the fork four hundred years ago outraged the public sentiment of his day. Riots took place over them, and at least one divine preached against them as unhallowed and disrespectful to the Deity. When the Pilgrim Fathers, from whom all Boston is descended, except the North End, landed on Plymouth Rock not one solitary fork bore testimony to the respectability with which it is evident they have been too hastily credited. Two hundred years ago nobody used a fork; to-day, nobody dares to use anything else. This perpetual control of mankind by itself, this constant and persistent demand for uniformity so irksome to all innovators, so repressing to all improvements, must be a terrible necessity. It shows by its very force how much the human race needs watching. . . .

We do not appreciate this tremendous searching omnipotent and omnipresent control of popular opinion because most of our lives are passed in easy submission to it. But it behooves a man to take heed before he begins to run counter to it, whether he longs to proclaim a great principle which will free a race, or merely wants to wear his hair long down his back. In most cases he will be simply suppressed, and even if he be of the stuff of which heroes are made he will many a time be sore of heart because he has seen fit to be unlike other men. . . .

What is this public sentiment? It is in its essence nothing more or less than the expression of the average intelligence and average ignorance of mankind. It demands, insists upon, and will have, uniformity. The race must go on together, and as a whole. It demands that those who are below the standard shall, in their outward lives, come up to the standard, and that those who are above the standard shall come down. . . . The reason why the race of man moves slowly is because it must move all together. The poor, the ignorant, the downtrodden are always saying to the rich and educated, inarticulately too often, but with a voice that brooks no denying, if you advance you must take us with you. . . .

Contributed by Robert S. Gallagher, who is writing a biography of Reed.

POSTSCRIPTS  TO HISTORY

COMMAGER ON COLLEGES

Of the nearly fourteen hundred senior colleges in the United States, more than eight hundred were founded in the nineteenth century. Considering that there were only two colleges in existence in the seventeenth century (Harvard, 1636; William and Mary, 1693) and but thirty-one more were established in the whole of the eighteenth century, the nineteenth century represented a tremendous leap forward in higher education. And throughout, the American college remained a unique institution. When unrest erupted a few years ago on campuses across the nation, Professor Henry Steele Commager of Amherst (founded 1821), a member of our advisory board and a frequent contributor, saw in that uniqueness the origins of modern student discontent. He described it in an essay, "The Crisis of the University," which appeared in the Long Island newspaper Newsday *in June of 1969. The professor's perspective is as pertinent today as it was then, and so we are herewith reprinting an excerpt with his and* Newsday's *kind permission.*

The phenomenon of student dissent in America has two clear dimensions, though the students themselves are aware of only one of them. Vertically it is rooted in some two centuries of American experience with colleges and universities, experiences quite different from those of Old World nations. Horizontally it reflects the pervasive frustration, outrage, and despair of the young at the Vietnam war, the draft, the armaments race, the destruction of the environment, racial injustice—at all that is implied in that epithet "the establishment."

It is that heritage that largely ex-plains why the revolt of youth against the establishment is directed toward the university rather than toward government, or parties, or the military, or Dow Chemical or Chase Manhattan or the Automobile Workers of America; it explains, too, why students who revolt against the university claim special exemption because they are part of the university, and demand that it protect them and care for their every need.

The university, as it emerged out of medieval Italy, France, and England and developed over the centuries, had three clear functions. The first was to train young men for essential professions: the church, the law and medicine, and perhaps teaching. The second was to preserve the heritage of the past, and pass it on to future generations intact. The third—first clarified by Göttingen and her sister universities in Germany in the eighteenth and nineteenth centuries—was to expand the boundaries of knowledge through research. The two ancient universities of England added a fourth which was never quite clear: to train a social elite to the tasks of governance.

Because the American colonials were unable to establish genuine universities, they created instead something quite new: the college— and the college remains, to this day, a unique American institution, occupying a twilight zone between the high school and the university. As American students were very young —boys went to Harvard or Pennsylvania or Yale at the age of twelve or thirteen, though a really bright lad like John Trumbull could pass the entrance examinations to Yale at the age of seven—they had to be treated as children: hence the early practice of *in loco parentis* and its persistence through the years and even the centuries. As they came from simple middle-class households, without (for the most part) learning or sophistication, they had to be taught elementary subjects, and the plan of study had to be laid out for them with utmost circumspection. Thus the long tradition, still very much with us, that the college is a kind of extension of the high school, that students must be taught everything in formal courses, and that students are intellectually, as well as socially and morally, *in statu pupillari.*

These characteristics of the American college persisted into the nineteenth century, and when, in the 1860's, Americans created their first universities, they established them not as substitutes for the colleges, but as continuations of the college, and adapted them, very largely, to collegiate rather than to university standards.

Just as the antecedents of the colleges had been Cambridge and Edinburgh, so the antecedents of the university were Göttingen and Berlin and Leipzig. But this could not last, or, where it did, it produced a kind of academic schizophrenia. Actually the university was bound to develop differently in a democratic and equalitarian society than in an aristocratic society. Because the United States did not have the scores of other institutions to carry on much of the work of science and research, or even of ordinary cultural activities (as did most Old World countries), almost everything that society wanted done in these areas was handed over to the university. Thus the schools of agriculture, of engineering, of library science, of nursing, of hotel management, of business administration, of almost anything that society or government wanted. Thus, too, came the multiversity, the university that did not confine itself merely to four faculties, nor to the traditional functions of professional training and research, but took on the most miscellaneous activities, academic and otherwise.

Thus by the twentieth century the special character of higher education in the United States was pretty well fixed. It was an education that was to be open to all, that was dominated by the collegiate idea, that inevitably took on the habits of *in loco parentis*. It was required to teach everything that society wanted taught, or that special-interest groups in society were strong enough to get taught; it was expected to acquiesce in the democratic notion that all subjects were equal; and it was expected to respond to all the demands of government or society, to serve these masters in every way that it could serve—as a sanctuary for the young, as a moral training ground, as a social and matrimonial agency, as a social-welfare center, as an agency for entertaining the community, as a center for research in all fields, and as a handmaiden of government. Some of the private institutions escaped the most onerous of these demands, but even they fell easily into the habit of accepting them.

This pattern of the college-university worked well enough as long as almost all elements in the community agreed on the basic assumptions that were implicit in it: that the uni-

versity was to "reflect" American life (the current formula is that its student body is supposed to be a reflection of the whole of American society), that it was to train character as well as the mind, that it was to inculcate all the going "values" of American life, that it was, in short, an integral part of the establishment, and that the establishment itself was sound, just, and enlightened. . . .

But it is not the business of the university to be relevant in the way that a newspaper or a television station is relevant. It is not the business of the university to allow itself to be captured by the immediate, the momentary, the sensational. The university has other relevancies. It is—or should be—relevant to the whole of the past and the whole of the future. It finds a place for scholars who think classical archaeology or the civilization of the Incas is relevant. It finds a place for those who are sure that there can be nothing more relevant than art, music, philosophy. It has, too, another very special function. It must create an atmosphere in which students can discover what is relevant to them, and provide the facilities for them to enlarge that relevance. For relevance is essentially subjective. It is something that happens to an individual as a result of experience. That experience may be hearing a Mozart trio, or solving a difficult problem in mathematics, or getting to know Voltaire or Goethe; it may be falling in love, or having a child, or writing a poem. Do the young really suppose that only Professor Herbert Marcuse or Stokely Carmichael are relevant, only sociology and black studies? All experience is against them, including their own.

The university is the most honorable and the least corrupt institution in American life. It is, with the church, the one institution that associates us with the past and the future, the one institution that has, through all our history, served, or

tried to serve, the interests of the whole of mankind and the interests of truth. No other institution can perform the functions that the university performs, no other can fill the place that it has for so long filled, and with such intellectual and moral affluence. If we destroy the university, we will destroy a unique institution. As the integrity of civilization depends in part on the university, we will be dealing an irreparable blow to a civilization now in moral peril.

REPEATING HISTORY

As this issue goes to press, Governor George Wallace of Alabama lies gravely wounded by bullets fired from the handgun of a would-be assassin while he was campaigning for the Presidential nomination in Maryland. It made us think, sadly, of this passage from an essay we published in October, 1970, by the late Richard Hofstadter, called "America as a Gun Culture":

"In 1968, after the assassinations of Robert F. Kennedy and Martin Luther King, Jr., there was an almost touching national revulsion against our own gun culture, and for once the protesting correspondence on the subject reaching senators and representatives outweighed letters stirred up by the extraordinarily efficient lobby of the National Rifle Association. And yet all that came out of this moment of acute concern was a feeble measure, immensely disappointing to advocates of serious gun control, restricting the mail-order sales of guns. It seems clear now that the strategic moment for gun controls has passed and that the United States will continue to endure an armed populace, at least until there is a major political disaster involving the use of guns."

EXIT LINES

About to die at the untimely age of forty-four in 1883, Dr. George Miller Beard, a Connecticut physician and pioneer in neurology, remarked: "I should like to record the thoughts of a dying man for the benefit of science, but it is impossible." And with those words, Dr. Beard passed beyond further speech. Regardless of their inner thoughts, we do at least know what many individuals uttered before giving up the ghost. Some were clear-headed, sensing perhaps that they were speaking for posterity; this may have been the case with Nathan Hale, whose well-chosen comment before being hanged is surely the best remembered of all. Others about to die were delirious, and their minds—like Robert E. Lee's when he called for A. P. Hill to bring up his troops—wandered back over past struggles. The following are last words attributed to twenty-three Americans. Some quotations may have been dressed up a little, but not by us.

Henry Ward Beecher (1813–1887):
"Now comes the mystery."

Mary Dyer (?–1660), *Quaker martyr and friend of Anne Hutchinson, on being asked at her execution whether an elder of the church should pray for her:*
"Nay, first a child; then a young man; then a strong man, before an elder of Christ Jesus."

Samuel Hopkins (1721–1803), *clergyman:*
"Oh, it is only my body; all is right in my soul."

Samuel Newman (1602–63), *clergyman:*
"Angels, do your office."

Giles Corey (ca. 1612–92), *Massachusetts colonist pressed to death for witchcraft:*
"Add more weight that my misery may be the sooner ended."

John Quincy Adams (1767–1848):
"It is the last of earth. I am content."

James Madison (1751–1836):
"I always talk better lying down."

Benjamin Franklin (1706–90):
"A dying man can do nothing easy."

Thomas Paine (1737–1809), *asked by his physician whether he wished to believe that Jesus is the son of God:*
"I have no wish to believe on that subject."

Daniel Webster (1782–1852):
"I still live!"*

John C. Calhoun (1782–1850):
"The South! The South! God knows what will become of her."

John Wilkes Booth (1838–65):
"Tell mother—tell mother—I died for my country."

John Brown (1800–59):
"I am ready at any time—do not keep me waiting."

J. Pierpont Morgan (1837–1913):
"Don't baby me so!"

P. T. Barnum (1810–91):
"How were the circus receipts today at Madison Square Garden?"

*According to an unauthenticated story, as Webster lay in his dying coma the doctor instructed his attendant to give him a spoonful of brandy every half-hour while he lived. When the clock chimed and the brandy was not immediately produced, the great man opened his eyes and uttered his last words as a reminder.

Cornelius Vanderbilt (1794–1877):
"Yes, yes, sing that for me. I am poor and needy."

Louisa May Alcott (1832–88):
"Thus far the Lord has led me on."

William Cullen Bryant (1794–1878):
"Whose house is this? What street are we in? Why did you bring me here?"

Henry D. Thoreau (1817–62):
"I leave this world without a regret."

O. Henry (William Sydney Porter, 1862–1910):
"Turn up the lights. I don't want to go home in the dark."

Damon Runyon (1884–1946):
"You can keep the things of bronze and stone and give me one man to remember me just once a year."

Rudolph Valentino (1895–1926):
"Don't pull down the blinds! I feel fine. I want the sunlight to greet me."

Hart Crane (1899–1932), *poet, as he jumped into the sea:*
"Good-by, everybody!"